DEFINING MOMENTS

....

Coping with the Loss of a Child

HERITAGE BUILDERS PUBLISHING
MONTEREY, CLOVIS CALIFORNIA

HERITAGE BUILDERS PUBLISHING
© 2016

First Edition 2016

Contributing Editor, Kate Crenshaw, Judy Warner
Cover Design, Rae House
Book Design, Nord Compo
Published by Heritage Builders Publishing
Clovis, Monterey California 93619
www.HeritageBuildersPublishing.com   1-888-898-9563

ISBN 978-1-942603-54-2

Printed and bound in United States of America

HERITAGE BUILDERS

Real-World Testimonials About Coping with the Loss of a Child

"No matter what age our children are when we lose them, the recurring theme shared by all who have buried a child is that of feeling alone and isolated in our grief. Breaking the silence surrounding child loss is one of the greatest movements of our time because when we know we aren't alone in our pain, we begin to experience hope and discover what many would call their "new normal." In sharing our stories, we give one another permission to grieve, but we also give one another hope and permission to experience joy again without the guilt. Throughout these stories, you'll find that life after losing a child can be like a mosaic; when you start to pick up the shattered pieces and put them together, something beautiful begins to emerge."

—Alicia Bertolero (mother of eight babies in Heaven)

"We lost our only daughter a few years ago. I noticed that my wife and I both grieved in different ways. She reached out, sought counseling, and leaned on family and friends. I seemed to suffer in silence. It was hard for me to process my anger and sadness of her sudden passing. Reading the stories of other parents who have gone through this journey was incredibly helpful in my own healing. I realized that many other families experienced grief that was even beyond my own comprehension. If they could survive their loss (or even losses), then it gave me hope that I might be able to find joy again without feeling guilt for those feelings. I suggest this book as a gift for any parent who has experienced the devastating loss of a child."

—Michael Susso (father to Amy)

DEDICATION

This book is dedicated to Carson Warner Kennedy. You were born a baby, died a hero, and are now an angel. Thank you for giving me the courage and purpose to write this book. I love and miss you every day, my sweet boy. I feel you with me always.

To my parents, John and Judy Warner, for your unconditional support and love, and being there for every single important moment of my life. I love you!

To my beautiful children, Kyla, Cole & Hudson Kennedy. You are my joy and reason for being here. You gave my life purpose and direction and made a mother out of me. I love you!

To Lloyd Edward Kennedy. Thank you for always supporting me, believing in me, and encouraging me to finish this book. I know that you are holding Carson in Heaven right now.

This book is dedicated to all of the children who lost their lives and to the families who continue to be their legacies.

ACKNOWLEDGEMENTS

....

I want to thank each of the courageous parents who shared their deeply personal stories with all of us. This book also honors each of our children, whose stories will help to inspire other families, help save countless lives, maybe restore a struggling relationship, and give others hope again.

There are some people in our lives who appear at our darkest hour and give us hope. They extol experience and wisdom. The spiritual equity that they invest in you makes you better and projects your life to a place you could only dream of. That person for me is Sherman Smith. My dear friend, my publisher, my mentor, thank you seems so small to say in exchange for so much. I am so grateful to have you in my life.

To Glenda Finn. I don't even know where to start with you. When I lost my baby, you saved my life by bringing me this one. You always knew it was meant for me. I will be eternally grateful for your giving birth to this amazing dream and always showing me faith in action. I would not be here without your love, support, guidance, encouragement and prayers for so many years. Thank you for always believing in me and seeing the vision of where we are going.

To my mom, Judy Warner, for your countless hours of editing, extra pair of eyes, and for going through this journey with me. You also lost Carson, so you understand the extension of grief and how it resonates through a strong family. Your insight, experience, faith, and guidance was truly a blessing in the final outcome of this book. I can't imagine going through this book process without you. You have always been there for me in the big moments of my life—for every moment of celebration, joy, heartache, and despair. I love you.

To Cookie Bakke, my earliest reader. Your generous encouragement, suggestions, and insight moved me forward, capturing the honesty in what I was struggling to share.

To Rick and Caroline Alfheim for responding to the voicemail that I left on the church's phone when I reached out for help many years ago. It was your direction that led me to great healing, resources, and also to the publisher of this book. I will always be grateful for your kindness and prayers. I have been so blessed beyond measure directly from your efforts and support.

To David Kennedy, Carson's father, who went on the same journey with me. Thank you for your courage and support that carried our family through its darkest hour.

When my life was on fire, most people were running away to save themselves. One person was brave enough to help me face my demons and dragons, and help contain the fire. Tom Kokoska, I will forever be grateful for your friendship, strength, and support when I had nothing to give in return.

Have you ever had an angel appear out of nowhere, a complete stranger, who knocks you off your feet and reminds you that you matter and your dreams matter? That person is Peter Muwaswes. Thank you for keeping me focused, accountable, and believing in myself when I had forgotten what it felt like to have hope again.

Jeff Brown, more than anyone besides my kids, you saw how hard I worked every single day to put this book together. You saw the raw emotions of speaking in depth with so many families for years about their own journey. When the process took its toll on my emotions, you were there to pick up the pieces. You always

Acknowledgements

offered encouragement to keep going. I will always appreciate you for that. You will always be my hero.

Kevin Lord, even though you feel you only threw a few grains of sand my way, you reminded me that I was building a beach. Thank you for your support, motivation, and for understanding whether I needed a pat on the head or a kick in the pants.

Endless thanks to each of you ~
Melanie

TABLE OF CONTENTS

Acknowledgments 9

Introduction 15

Chapter One: **Creating a Cause** 21
    Believe What Your Heart Says, Lois Duncan 21
    A Message to Violent Criminals, Mike Reynolds ... 25
    My Life's Detour, Gloria Horsley 29
    The Gigantic Mattress, Dick & Sandy Gallagher 35
    Miracle in Disguise, Dean Eller 38

Chapter Two: **Power of Forgiveness** 47
    A Journey to Forgiveness, Dianne Rogers 47
    To Forgive, Not Forget, Martha Tessmer 56
    Molly Day, Doug Griffin 60
    Two Angels, One Life, Melanie Warner 67
    Just One Life, Violeta Astilean 74

Chapter Three: **Angel Babies** 81
    Seeds of Hope, Cookie Bakke 81
    Incompatible With Life, Shari Savage 87
    The Grief Letter, Jill Hammond Jackson 91
    Three Days, Jennifer Davis 94
    I'll Hold You in Heaven, Charisse Jimenez 100
    The Grateful Eight, Alicia Bertolero 105

Chapter Four: **Living With Hope** 111
    A Happy Seed, Danielle Lawhead 111
    The Sweetest Thing, Dan Cope 115

Terminal Hope, Juanita Arroyo 119

A New Angel, Megan Shank 124

The Smile That Warms Your Heart, Celine Ford ... 127

A Life's Journey, Patrick Murphy 132

Chapter Five: **Sudden Shock** 137

Tolerating Shrapnel, Janet Burroway 137

My Only Child, Steve Roberts 145

The Power of Choices, Debbi Rath 150

The Next Generation, Cecilia DiNunno 156

When Can I Go Home? Mary Johnson 159

The Michael Tree, Clara Hinton 162

Chapter Six: **Faith and Prayer** 167

The Brave One, Michelene Fitzgerald 167

Lost and Found, Eddie Rivera 171

Just For Today, Karen Tesi 177

On a Mission, Dale West 181

My Friends Need Jesus, Cindy Brown 184

Chapter Seven: **Gifts From Beyond** 191

The Unexpected Gift, Irene Freitas 191

The Gratitude Letter, Joanie Cook 197

Celestial Conversations, Lo Anne Mayer 201

New Life For Others, Lisa A. Bright 205

Chapter Eight: **Multiple Losses** 211

Walking Through the Fire, Brad & Jan Lopez 211

When Four Becomes One, Elly Sutherland 217

Making a Family God's Way, Cora Merkley 219

Unexpected Journey, Gretchan Wheeler 231

Faith Through Fog, Renee Vigil 236

Meet The Author 243

Share Your Story 245

INTRODUCTION

....

There is no doubt that it goes against the natural order of the universe to bury a child. If you are reading this book, then it means you are in a lot of pain. I am so very sorry for your loss. I know you have probably heard that phrase so many times by now, and it sounds benign compared to the pain you are experiencing, but I can tell you that there is hope. There is a way to heal.

I've been through it with my own son, Carson Warner Kennedy. Nothing prepares you for the death of a child, especially when it's unexpected. He was born in my arms, and he died in my arms. Full circle. It was one of the most painful, horrifying, helpless, yet strangely beautiful and spiritual moments of my life.

Through my own process, I learned the key to healing that I hope you would find in this book. I learned to be grateful for the experience of having such an extraordinary human being pass through me into this world and be there for every moment of his brief life and see the amazing purpose not only of his life, but my own. As mothers, we play the significant role of being the gatekeepers to the world. Our purpose is to literally push our kids out into the world, eventually letting them go, inch by inch, day by day, until they are able to survive on their own and fulfill their own purpose in life.

It's been estimated that over fourteen million children under the age of five die every year. Those staggering numbers leave behind many people who are hurting. Research has shown us that after the death of a child, families struggle with a high risk of divorce, drugs, alcohol abuse, and even suicide to lessen the burden of the seemingly endless despair of this type of tragedy.

So what is the solution? There isn't just one. For me, since I almost died at the same time my son did, it created a spiritual shift, a desire to do better, to be better. I decided to live my life with purpose and not just go through the business of life. That was the gift my son gave me.

I found ways to honor my son in the way that I chose to live the rest of my life. Instead of choosing the path of downward spiral, I made a conscious choice to walk through the pain. I learned that there were several stages I had to go through in order to heal my heartache, but eventually I learned to find joy again—without feeling guilty. I learned that the length of time I mourned his death had nothing to do with the depth of love I feel for my son.

When your child dies, it changes you forever. It can make you bitter or it can make you better. Thank you to my mentor, Gary Zukav, for teaching me these incredible words of healing for anyone else who is grieving the loss of a loved one:

"When a parent loses a child, the grief is a matter of perspective: the perspective of the personality or the perspective of the soul. From the perspective of the soul, interactions between personalities are meaningful and every soul comes into the earth's school when it chooses and every soul leaves the earth's school when it chooses.

If you look at Carson as a personality who lived for a short time, then encountered tragic circumstances and died, then you are looking from a point from a personality. If you look at Carson as a soul, like yourself, like everyone else on this Earth that left this Earth when it chose, you will have a different perspective.

You will be able to see the gifts this soul offered to you in its short stay on Earth. You will reach a place in your life where you are grateful that this soul chose to be with you for however short a time. If you do not, you will live your life in anguish thinking a tragedy has occurred.

When your other kids have birthdays, graduations, you will say, "Carson should have been here." Through all of this time, you will be imposing on your other kids a burden to carry because no matter what they do or how successful they are, it will be causing mommy or daddy pain.

If you look at Carson as a great soul like yourself who voluntarily left it, in order to be with you and offer gifts, then you will begin the process to be grateful for the power of the interaction that you had with that soul and to be able to receive the gifts that soul came here specifically to give you and his siblings. If you do not, you will continually be turning away those gifts. You will be denying the very wealth of wisdom and compassion that was offered to you by this soul."

Another thing that helped me cope was to talk with other parents who were going through the same pain. When I started hearing their stories, I remember thinking that their story was worse than mine. If you ask them, they would say that someone else's story was worse than theirs. A loss is a loss and affects everyone differently.

The process of healing is different for everyone. But there was a comfort in seeing other people survive it and hearing how they walked through that dark journey and survived it intact. The last thing I wanted was someone else telling me what I was supposed to feel, especially someone who never lost a child. I realized that I had joined a club that no one wanted to join, and I would be a lifetime member.

Initially, I began to share those stories in a local magazine that I owned in California. Two months after Carson passed away, we ran a story that included a few families who had lost a child and the messages of hope that they could pass along to other families who were suffering.

Parents Dick and Sandy Gallagher (their story is in this book) were featured in the magazine story. They shared how their son, David, had died of suicide as a teenager. The story ran in December 2005.

In February 2006, I was walking through a restaurant and a woman stopped me and broke down in tears. She told me how she had read the article and their message about suicide prevention had resonated with her and her husband. They decided to take their son away to the mountains for a weekend after reading the story. It was mid-December. By the end of the weekend, their son revealed to them that he and ten of his friends had planned a suicide pact for Christmas Day. . . a mere ten days later.

They were able to get in touch with the other parents, talk with counselors and the school, and prevent it completely. All of those kids are still alive today, and some are even married with their own kids.

I will never forget the look in her eyes when she looked directly at me and asked, "What would have happened if you had run that story in January?" At that very moment, I realized that Carson's life (and his death, that inspired the story) had indirectly just saved the lives of ten teenagers.

Another story we featured was Dianne Rogers (also in this book). Her young son, Sean, had been killed, and she was reluctant to share her very personal story. I urged her to share it in our article as I felt strongly that a parent would read her story and maybe it would give them hope. I told her that I specifically felt it might even prevent a parent from committing suicide.

Her story ran in the magazine. She lives in San Diego, California but happened to be traveling to Fresno, California (where the article ran locally). She was flying to Fresno to look at property. The real estate agent who was supposed to pick her up got stuck in an escrow emergency and called out to a young man in the office who was walking by. It was a random request to go pick up his client at the airport and take her to look at houses.

That young man drove to the airport, picked up Dianne, and they started talking about life as he drove her around to look at houses. The more she talked, the more it sounded familiar. At one point, he pulled the car over, stared at her and asked, "Are you the woman from the magazine story? The one who lost her son?" She was surprised that he would know her, but answered, "Yes."

The man burst into tears and said, "My sister died six months ago. I have been so distraught and unable to move forward. I had seriously been contemplating suicide. I had planned it—a date and everything. Then I read your story about your son. I realized that if you can move forward in your life, after such a horrible loss, then there is hope for me."

Dianne was floored as she shared such a sacred moment with this random stranger, recalling the conversation we had had about how her story might impact others. I saw it as another way that Carson's life, and now Sean's life, had just saved someone else's.

Another story that had been featured in the magazine was Dean Eller's story. His daughter, Jenny, had died of a rare blood disorder (and is also in this book). A few years after the story ran, a woman approached me at the grocery store and told me that the story had convinced her to start donating blood. She and her mom had started donating blood together, and both became organ donors. Shortly after that, her mother was in a horrible car accident and passed away. But she was so proud of the fact that her mother's organs saved the lives of several other people, and she had donated gallons of blood to the local blood bank—all because of that article. Another way that Carson's life and Jenny's life had impacted and saved other lives.

When I was pregnant with my last son, Hudson, I had gone to Macy's to buy shoes. It was the heat of summer, and I was eight months pregnant. When I got home, I discovered that, somehow, the salesclerk had put two different shoes in the box. So I had to drive my big, pregnant self back to the store—in 110-degree heat. I wasn't very happy.

The minute I walked into the store, I grabbed the first person I saw who worked there and told her what had happened. The woman proceeded to tell me that the story we had written a few years back was still on her fridge. That story about parents who had lost a child had motivated her to adopt a child. It was something she had always wanted to do, but the story inspired her to take those steps. She showed me a photo of her little baby whom she had recently adopted. If the shoes had not been messed up, I would never have heard that story. That sole story turned into another soul story.

Once again, I saw the impact of Carson's life on others. I had no idea the ripple effect these stories would have on so many people. That is what inspired this book. I hope you find some peace within these pages. Know that it was made with love, positive intentions, and the true hope that it will inspire you to be able to see the purpose in your child's life and your own, to focus on their life, not just their death.

I hope that you find comfort, solace, and healing in these pages. I want to thank all of the courageous parents who shared their emotional, painful, searing stories in order to accomplish the purest intention of helping you through your own journey.

May you be blessed as you continue living your own life. Just know that if you look for the reason why your child died, you will rarely, if ever, find an answer that satisfies you. Asking "why" always holds us back. Instead, if you look hard enough, you will find the purpose, not only in your child's life, but also in your own. There is a lesson that will help you grow. Start by asking, "What can I learn from this experience? Where do I go from here? How can I find a place that allows me to feel joy for my child who died the same way I feel happiness and joy when I see my other children?"

May God bless you on your journey and bring peace to your broken heart.

Melanie Warner

....

CHAPTER ONE

CREATING A CAUSE

Believe What Your Heart Says
By Lois Duncan

My husband and I are members of the Club That Nobody Wants to Join. The dues are high and there are no benefits. In that, we and our fellow club members are alike.

That's not to say that we've all had the same experiences. For some our child never had a chance to draw one breath. For some our child went to sleep one night and for some unknown reason never woke up. Some of our children died from illnesses or accidents. Others caused their own deaths, either unintentionally or deliberately, (and those deaths may be the hardest of all to bear.)

In our case, the cause was murder.

The call from the emergency room of the University of New Mexico Hospital came just before midnight. The caller said our daughter, Kaitlyn Arquette, 18, was there and had been injured but would give out no further information over the phone. We threw on our clothes, leaped into the car, and drove to the hospital, running red lights all the way.

My husband dropped me off at the door while he took the car across to the visitors' parking lot. The nurse who had called us was standing in wait in the doorway, and I knew that it had to be bad when she took me in her arms.

"A car wreck?" I couldn't conceive of any other possibility.

"Your daughter's been shot in the head," the nurse said quietly. "She's in a coma. You need to prepare yourself for the fact that you may lose her."

Twenty hours later we allowed Kait to be removed from life support so her organs could be transplanted. In that way, she saved five lives, so her own short life was given meaning. We knew she would have wanted that.

Twenty-five years have now passed since that hideous night. I have very few memories of Kait's funeral. I've blocked out all recollection of the service—the coffin being lowered into that hole in the ground—the gathering afterwards. That's how we protect ourselves. Some self-defense mechanism kicks in to save us. If that doesn't happen, we either die or go insane.

My husband and I, and our surviving children, will never be the same people we were before. I won't try to dole out advice on all aspects of grieving, but there's one particular piece of advice I'd like to share because it's seldom talked about.

Don't believe everything well-meaning people tell you. BELIEVE WHAT YOUR HEART TELLS YOU.

Those well-meaning people may include your relatives, your spiritual advisor, your psychiatrist, or your best friends. They're trying to help you, but they're doing so from their own perspectives.

If what they tell you goes against your instincts, don't accept it. The person to trust is YOURSELF.

Immediately after Kait's murder, the hospital sent a grief counselor to our home. In an effort to reassure us, he said, "Don't assume that you're crazy if you hear your child's voice in the night. That illusion is experienced by the majority of people who are grieving the loss of a child."

I accepted that statement.

UNTIL IT HAPPENED TO ME. I had just gone to bed and was nowhere near to sleep, when Kait's voice spoke directly into my left ear. It was just as real as if she was kneeling next to the bed. She didn't say, "Mother, I love you," or any of the other sweet fuzzy things I would have given my life to hear. She said, "Look at my phone bill."

I was in the process of settling her affairs—paying bills, settling credit card debts, and so on. I hadn't yet opened her phone bill. The next morning I did, and instead of automatically paying it, I reviewed her long distance calls.

When I did that, I discovered two calls to California, made from Kait's supposedly unoccupied apartment, minutes after she was pronounced brain dead. I dialed the numbers, but both had been disconnected.

I gave them to the police, who said they couldn't trace them, because they were unlisted. But an investigative reporter was able to do that. The numbers turned out to be the home and beeper numbers for the head of an interstate crime ring that Kait was in a position to expose.

Her boyfriend and his friends were part of that crime ring, and Kait was breaking up with that boyfriend on the night of her murder. The boyfriend was with us at the hospital when Kait died, but he raced down the corridor to a phone and apparently called his friends, who must have been waiting in Kait's apartment. One of those friends made the calls to California.

That led to our realization that there were layers to this nightmare that went far beyond the "random drive-by shooting" that police were insisting on calling it.

That kind of experience has continued to occur off and on throughout all the years that our family has conducted our personal investigation of Kait's murder. When I hear Kait's voice—occasionally when I'm awake but most often in dreams— and it gives me specific information, I ask our private investigator to follow up on it.

Amazingly, this has led to important discoveries.

Maybe that's just coincidence, but maybe it isn't.

I've spoken with many parents who have heard their dead child's voice. On many occasions, it probably WAS an illusion, created by grief-befuddled minds. But there also exists the possibility that it wasn't.

One mother was actually able to laugh when she told me about her experience, because it sounded so ridiculous. This woman was highly religious and went to church every day, praying for communication from her deceased teenage son. That never happened, not even in a dream.

Then one morning she was vacuuming her living room and her son's voice shouted, "Hey, Ma!"

"I was stunned," she told me. "And, believe it or not, I was furious. 'Damn it, Peter!' I yelled. 'For five years I've been begging to hear from you, and now, when I do, all you have to say is 'Hey, Ma'! Then I burst into tears and fell on my knees in gratitude. Grief makes us react in crazy ways."

"So you truly believe that was Peter?" I asked her hesitantly.

"No doubt about it," she said. "It sounded just like him. He never liked being told what to do. And he always called me Ma."

The bottom line is: WE are the parents of these children. We know them better than anyone else in the world. Their fathers planted the seeds that caused them to exist. Their mothers were physically linked to them for nine whole months, and both are emotionally linked to them forever.

It's up to US to decide what is and isn't real, and that knowledge is embedded in our hearts.

Lois Duncan is the author of over fifty books, ranging from children's books to teenage suspense novels like *I Know What You Did Last Summer* and *Down A Dark Hall*. But the two that are "books from her heart" are adult non-fiction: *Who Killed My Daughter?* and *One To The Wolves: On The Trail Of A Killer*, about her family's struggles to solve the murder of their youngest child, Kaitlyn Arquette. Lois has been keynote speaker for a national convention of The Compassionate Friends and has helped dozens of other families of murdered children write accounts of their own children's murders to keep those stories from becoming buried and forgotten because the cases have gone "cold." For more info, visit: loisduncan.arquettes.com

A Message to Violent Criminals
By Mike Reynolds

Our daughter, Kimber, had driven back home from college for the weekend to be a bridesmaid in a friend's wedding. I was a wedding photographer and was at the same wedding taking photos. I watched her walk down the aisle, and all I could think about was her own wedding someday. I questioned how well I would hold up if I had to give her away.

I was sitting next to an old friend whose daughter had died sixteen months earlier in a car accident. I wondered how he must have felt watching someone else's daughter walk down the aisle knowing that he would never have that experience. And I thought to myself, but for the grace of God, that could be me.

Kimber had planned to drive back to Los Angeles on Sunday, but a leaking radiator delayed her return another day, so she decided to leave Tuesday morning instead.

On Monday night, although our city was in a severe drought, there was a cloudburst of rain and it started to pour. For some reason, I started to think about how Kimber was born on a rainy day and so was I. We were even born in the same delivery room at the same hospital. Both of our boys were born on a rainy day. And Sharon and I were married on a rainy day. For whatever reason, I had always thought I would die a violent death on a rainy day. Don't ask my why; it was just something I was sure of.

The previous December, a young man had been murdered in a nice part of town after Christmas shopping for his family. The murder had a profound effect on my wife, Sharon. From that point on, Sharon had a growing apprehension each time the kids were home. It was especially noticeable when Kimber was home. Instead of being the happy, excited Mom, it was like she was nervous and couldn't wait for the kids to leave. She even questioned herself as a mother at times for feeling that way.

That night, Kimber decided to go get some dessert with a friend. She borrowed her mom's boots and topped off her look with my checkered sports jacket. "How do I look?" she asked me. I told her she looked great. I didn't realize it would be the last time I would ever talk with her. I was exhausted and went to bed about 10:45 p.m. Had I stayed up a few minutes later, I would have seen the 11:00 p.m. news showing that a young woman had been shot at a local restaurant.

At exactly 10:41 p.m., Kimber and her friend Greg walked to their car in a popular and crowded neighborhood in Fresno. Two men on a stolen motorcycle appeared out of nowhere and pinned Kimber against the car. One had a gun. He grabbed her purse; she slightly resisted. In front of Greg and all the patrons of the restaurant, he shot her in the head at point blank range. She was just four months shy of her nineteenth birthday.

At 2:30 a.m. we were awakened with a phone call that every parent fears, but never wants to receive. It was her friend, Greg. He had come to the house, rung the doorbell, called many times—yet we didn't wake up.

I heard Sharon say, "Kimber's been shot? In the head? Where is she?"

When we arrived at the hospital, we weren't prepared for what we would see. Nothing can prepare you for the sight of your baby girl hooked up to machines and ventilators. How could this be the same girl who just helped me hang wallpaper and wrap a Christmas gift for her mom a few hours earlier?

We did what we could. We prayed and kept talking to her in hopes that she could hear us. We started notifying family and friends and summoned them to come to the hospital.

The hospital did everything they could. Another twenty-four hours went by, and her conditioned worsened. It became apparent that Kimber's fight for life was nearing its end.

Each family member took their private moment with Kimber to say their final goodbyes. Then it was my turn. At this point, Kimber was still attached to life support systems, and the doctors had assured us that, due to massive brain trauma, she was already gone. I walked over to her bed and kissed her on the forehead. One eye opened!

The doctors told us it was a reflexive motion, but I believe it was Kimber giving one last effort to signal me, to let me know that she knew I was there. I whispered to her my promise that I would find the men who did this to her and justice would be served.

Twenty-six hours after she was shot, Kimber Reynolds died. My premonition that I would die a violent death on a rainy day had been tragically borne out for my daughter.

On the way home from the hospital, Sharon began to ask, "How can I ever have a Christmas tree again? Because Kimber always decorated it with me. How could I not have a Christmas tree? Kimber would be so disappointed."

A few hours after her death, I received a call from a local radio station. I realized that the only way we would find the men who killed her was to make an appeal right away. The longer we waited, the greater the chance was that they would get away.

We talked about the details of the crime and how important it was for people to know that this happened in a busy area, in a nice neighborhood, in cold blood. I made a prediction that the person who committed this crime was probably in trouble many times. My guess is whatever went wrong with this person, probably happened when he was a kid.

By the time the broadcast was over, the police received a tip from an informant who said they knew who the killer was. He had mentioned it to some friends. Now we had a positive identification and just had to locate him. As it turned out, both men involved in the shooting had a long history with violent crimes, multiple offenses, and drugs.

One of the suspects was located and killed in a police shoot out. The other one was caught days later and a hearing was set. At the trial, it was revealed that the gunman had his first offense for trafficking heroin at eleven years old. He had only known a life of crime and had been a revolving door, in and out of prison. He tried to plea bargain his case and was sentenced to only four years for the murder of Kimber Reynolds. This is when I knew the law had to change.

When I thought about the promise I made to Kimber the night she died, I didn't feel that justice had been served. Even though one was dead, the other one was going to be free to take another victim in a few short years.

Some people question whether talk radio is worthwhile or ever accomplishes something. You better believe it does. It helped identify and catch the men who murdered my daughter, and it eventually delivered the issue of the need to change the law for repeat offenders.

I knew something had to change. I formed a small focus group to strategize. Of all the problems in the criminal justice world, what single thing could we do that would have the most impact?

Right away, we focused our sights on repeat offenders. We researched and learned that nearly 70% of all crime was committed by only 6% of criminals. It was the violent ones who continued to commit crimes every time they were on the street.

I began to take the issue to the public and appeal for their help. I began working with local legislators to define a law that would keep repeat offenders in prison. We decided it would be called

"Three Strikes." People understood and could grasp the concept of three strikes and you're out. It basically said if you commit a serious or violent crime, the third time, you would go to prison for life.

It took years and a long journey to get it on the ballot, not to mention miracles along the way, but eventually it was passed into a law in California. When they saw crime statistics dropping, other states began to adopt the law. Currently, twenty-eight states have gone on to create their own version of "Three Strikes."

Twenty-one months after her death, I had kept my promise to Kimber. I think about the power of that promise every day. How else could a simple wedding photographer manage to have changed the entire criminal justice system?

Mike Reynolds launched the Three Strikes Law in California as a direct result of his daughter's murder from repeat offenders. It has since sparked a nationwide proliferation of measures and voter initiatives that prompted the federal government to pass a law that imposes the three strikes punishment standard on anyone committing violent federal offenses. What Mike initiated as a personal homage to his daughter has become a lightening rod for citizen action groups across the country. He continues to work on passing (and protecting) other laws related to prison sentences and violent crimes involving guns. www.threestrikes.org

My Life's Detour
By Gloria Horsley

I woke early this morning to the sound of a driving rainstorm. I was planning on golfing this morning, but rain has given me the opportunity to write this promised essay. As I put on my robe and head for my home office, I thought how ironic it is that a downpour is giving me the time to write about another driving rainstorm that would change my life forever.

The date was April 2, 1983. Two young men, each seventeen-years-old, were returning from a movie and pizza at Tyson's corner in Arlington, Virginia. My son, Scott, was a passenger in the car driven by his cousin, Matthew, who was driving his prized 1968 Camaro.

According to the police report, two witnesses said the Camaro suddenly spun out of control as it was preparing to exit the freeway, hydroplaned, and crashed into a bridge abutment. The witnesses, who were returning from a performance of *Oklahoma*, jumped from their car to help the boys, but the car suddenly burst into flames and the rest is history.

Two young men, alcohol-free, wearing seat belts, were instantly engulfed by the flames and burned to death, changing the lives of two families forever.

Forever Changed

Yes, I said my life was forever changed, but I did not say it was destroyed. On that horrible day, tragedy took not only Scott's life but put my life on an unexpected detour.

This detour put me on bumpy roads, many of which I would never have traveled. However, in many ways it has been an amazing trip. Let me share with you a bit of my path from pain and hurt to the fulfilling life I have today. It is my hope that you will find one or two things in my story that will aid you on your journey.

Year One

For me year one was a frozen year. I was brittle and just going through the motions. I was the psychiatric nursing consultant to the University of Rochester Medical Center and taught at the nursing school. In my consulting job I covered the medical and surgical services. This included the ICU and the burn unit. I was familiar with car accidents and often worked with patients and nurses in the burn unit and in the ICU.

I returned to work three weeks after Scott was killed and found a mixed bag of co-workers and friends who could deal with the death of a colleague's child. Although Scott was burned to death, no one on the burn unit mentioned his cause of death. The boys luckily never got to the ICU. I say, "luckily" because recovering from severe burns is a long, painfully brutal process and not always successful.

I was fairly well versed in responses to sudden death. Only a few days earlier, I was called to the hospital room of a young man who had rolled his van, killing his fourteen-year-old brother. At the time I told his parents, "I don't know what you are going through, but I may have some things that can help you."

It was ironic that only a few days later I found those words to be prophetic and discovered that I had no idea the physical and emotional toll the death of a child takes. I knew the literature describing normal responses to sudden loss, and now I was experiencing it through my own personal loss. It was like being given a road map and told you had no choice but to take the trip. No turning back.

Below are some of the things I experienced. You might recognize some of them in yourself.

Taking The Trip

With the words, "they are both dead," ringing in my ears came an adrenaline rush that was like hitting a brick wall. I lost five pounds in three days due to the adrenaline rush.

Responding to the deaths over the weeks and months, I threw what I can only describe as one giant tantrum. I had always believed that if you wanted something badly enough you could get it. I had waves of grief wash over me; I never knew when the tsunami would hit.

I yearned and searched for Scott every place we had been together. I actually got a stiff neck from looking. It was a relief that first summer to rent a house in a place he had never been.

At times I was irritable. I had insomnia and nightmares. I felt responsible for his death. "Why," I asked myself, "hadn't I let him take my car as I had the night before?" I had trouble matching my socks. It took me hours to get ready for work. Crying and screaming in forty-five minute showers was the norm. I had thoughts of wanting to be united with him and, at times, had thoughts that he really hadn't died.

Year Two

I made it through year one only to find that year two was no picnic. I felt some relief and even pride that I had gotten through the firsts of everything: first holidays, first birthdays, and now the death day. I invited a group of Scott's friends to our house for pizza on April 2nd. This wasn't for everyone. My husband and younger daughter, Heather, chose not to join us in what I saw as a celebration of Scott's life. Our daughters Heidi and Rebecca were in college; I am not sure what they did.

The second year was tough. At times, I thought I was going crazy. I wasn't really crazy; I was just thawing out after the big freeze. I was beginning to accept the fact that Scott wasn't coming back and this would be my life.

I felt fragile and became overly competent at work in order to cover up my pain. Eventually, I decided that I needed to leave the hospital and the medical center.

I felt it was necessary to move forward rather than just collapse, so I decided to return to graduate school. I chose

Syracuse University, which was a two-hour drive from our home in Rochester. It felt good to go someplace I had never been and to meet a new group of friends. This is not to say that I didn't take all my grieving patterns with me.

As my father-in-law always said, "Where the crow flies, the tail follows." Time is the one constant variable found in healing from loss. I was early in my grief, and it was helpful to find people who gave me a new audience with whom to share my story.

Year Three and Beyond

Telling my entire story would take a book, but I found that in the third year I began to smile and laugh again more easily. Guilt and shame lessened.

One of the benefits of having the worst happen was that I was less fearful and more adventuresome. I tried many things over the years, some more helpful than others. I went on silent retreats and vision quests, became a Reiki master, and started my current yoga practice. I met some amazing people and had some profound experiences.

I taught for Carolyn Myss, and learned about life contracts, energy healing, and archetypes. I became a friend and teacher of *The Work of Byron Katie*. Katie taught me that suffering was holding to the idea that Scott shouldn't have died. As Katie says, "argue with reality and you lose every time."

I learned about my grief behaviors by studying the Enneagram, a personality typing system, under the tutelage of Helen Palmer and David Daniels. I received a master's degree at the *Academy of Intuition Medicine* with Francesca McCartney.

Today I'm seeking not for knowledge or answers, but for an opportunity to give back to those who helped me on the journey of grief and recovery. With my family's help and support we started the not-for-profit Open to Hope Foundation.

We named it Open to Hope because we want to help those who have suffered a profound loss find a way to open their hearts to the idea that there may be hope again—the same hope we searched for and found when we lost our Scott.

Through Open to Hope we partner with The Compassionate Friends and founded a TCF chapter in Burlingame, California. Through The Compassionate Friends we have met many wonderful people and found that the death of a child really puts things into perspective. Supporting others in the healing process transcends all other issues; ego has no place and love abounds.

If you have lost a child, try to reach out. Find a group or join us at Open to Hope. Early on, let others serve you. Later on, you will find, as I have, that the final healing comes with serving others.

Guess what! The sun just came out, and I am going golfing with my husband.

God bless,

Dr. Gloria

Gloria C. Horsley MFC CNS Ph.D. is a bereaved parent and president of the Open to Hope Foundation. She is a clinical member of the American Association of Marriage and Family Therapy and a past faculty member of the University of Rochester School of Nursing. Gloria co-hosts with her daughter Dr. Heidi Horsley the award-winning cable television and radio shows *Open to Hope*. She blogs for the Huffington Post and Mother's Against Drunk Driving (MADD) and has authored a number of books and articles. She dedicates her work to her deceased son, Scott. Visit her at www.opentohope.com

The Gigantic Mattress
By Dick and Sandy Gallagher

> *"And thy own soul a sword shall pierce that the thoughts of many hearts may be revealed"* Luke 2:35

September is such a fickle month in the Central Valley of California. It can promise cool breezes that wipe the sweat off our long hot summers. Today it will disappoint as the forecast calls for temperatures above 100 degrees. But as Dick and I floated off to the kitchen at 5:00 a.m., it was a soft morning and still dark. It was September 18, 1984, just an ordinary day.

Our oldest, Mary Anne, age 23, had just moved out to her first apartment, and our son, Christopher, was away at UC Davis studying for his aeronautical/mechanical engineering degrees. Danny, at age 19, was at Fresno State working toward his teaching credential; 17-year old David was two weeks into his senior year in high school, and our youngest, Barbara, 15, was a sophomore.

Dan was the first one home that day and, noticing the air conditioner was cranking out cool air with windows open, he went back to David's room to close the window. He noticed something red on the screen, thinking that probably some kids threw tomatoes from the garden. Looking down, he saw David lying on the ground. He ran through the house, screaming, and out to the garden, where he found his brother dead from a gunshot wound to the head.

No words in the dictionary can describe the horror Dan witnessed or the life-long sorrow this action of suicide brought to our family and community. There were no warnings, no signs of depression, and no hint of a troubled spirit and soul. We had no clue and, honestly, couldn't even spell the word "suicide," much less envision it touching our family.

How could this beautiful child, who always had a joke to tell, always had a smile behind those eyes and was known for his sweetness and kindness, choose to end the music of that life? How do we go on, missing our redheaded, freckle-faced dear one every day and hour for the rest of our lives? And then, when do we wash his clothes for the final time, erasing his scent forever?

Each day after *that day* was like living on another planet, in another dimension where everything was pain and nothing seemed familiar or kind or good. As the months went by, we would count the days since the last morning we saw David. It was as if our world had stopped at that moment. David was alive last Tuesday; then it was six months since David died. It was like a raw wound, but unlike the bleeding kind, it didn't heal on its own with a Band-Aid.

On this planet, there was something resembling a toxic soup composed of anger, guilt, hopelessness, and the haunting question: why? Why did he do it? There was the fear that this pain could possibly encourage suicide by one of our other children. We lived in our past where our family was complete, but even there, sadness covered precious memories. There would always be someone missing in our family photos, at family events, every holiday, every birthday. How do we function as a family? Where do we walk to now?

This is not just a story about suicide and a family left behind to cope with unanswered questions and pain. It's more a story about God's *grace*. This is a story about the ultimate loss, the loss of a child to suicide, and what *grace* did about that.

Through all the fog and pain of grief there appeared a gigantic mattress made up of the hands, minds, voices, and the pain of others who have suffered a loss through a suicide death that caught us when we fell. There were angels in the form of our close-knit faith family, our friends, neighbors, our church, and community at large that held us up when we fell. There was the wisdom of advice to seek counseling for the entire family, as we knew it was way over our heads. We needed understanding. We needed to hear from other families who had survived the loss of a child or understood our pain. We were given in great abundance what we never dreamed we would ever need.

Grace gave us the strength we felt from each other as father and mother, husband and wife. Men and women grieve differently, but somehow, someway, we were able to see each other as best friends, leaning on each other for support and not blaming. Only grace can do that when you are at the pit of despair, fear, and doubt. It was like some sort of emotional and spiritual glue that kept us focused, enabling us to cooperate with God in His plan for our futures.

There was an early passion to *do something* about this tragic loss of life. The passion overrode the staggering depression we swam through and enabled *action.* Grace came in the form of others who came forward to join us in forming Fresno Survivors of Suicide Loss, which was founded in 1986 with the very first support group meeting. Those monthly meetings have been offered uninterrupted through the years.

We now have a dynamic executive director and board who serve this effort of helping in the healing of survivors and educating our community about depression, how to identify it, and how to get help. We learned that the majority of suicides occur because of untreated depression. We felt that if we could alert people to look for signs of depression, then it might encourage others to get help before they felt overcome by it.

Grace also came in the form of several leaders of a small mountain community who called us to come and just sit and talk about what had become the third leading cause of death among our youth. From that initial talk with those community leaders, the education program was formed. Helping us as well was a decision by our local ABC affiliate to present a documentary in prime time called *Desperate Measures,* which won an award from our local Mental Health Association.

The outreach expanded to a suicide prevention education program with survivor-driven presentations given to junior and senior high schools, senior organizations, first responders, nursing staff, law enforcement, and the professional world with the life-affirming message of our program: "QPR"—Question, Persuade, Refer.

These efforts have reached an estimated 100,000 individuals throughout these twenty-seven years. Minds and hearts have been enlightened; lives have been nurtured, uplifted, offered a hope for healing and the knowledge of the power of the choice to seek help for suicidal ideas and take action by seeking counseling and, perhaps, medication.

The reward of knowing that so many people have potentially been spared the pain we had to endure helps us see the grace from our own situation. Helping other people understand suicide has also helped in our own healing over the years. We understand the purpose and mission of David's life in our own through these stories, and we can see God at work.

Our heroes are the supporters and movers of Fresno S.O.S., the team members who present the education programs and facilitate our monthly meetings—each voice that has and will come forward, offering hearts and arms to comfort others on healing's journey, and an executive director who is a visionary, who gives selflessly and passionately to our goals.

To God be the glory!

Dick and Sandy Gallagher started Fresno S.O.S, a non-profit organization that spoke to schools, churches, and other organizations throughout the world on the warning signs of suicide. They spent over thirty years educating countless students and parents on the warning sides of suicide. For more information visit: www.fresnosos.org

Miracle in Disguise
By Dean Eller

How do you define a miracle?

Lately, I have noticed an abundance of faith-based movies in the theaters.

Heaven is for Real and *Miracles from Heaven* come to mind. I like these movies where a loved one is extremely sick, and a family's faith is stretched to the breaking point and even beyond. Then God steps in, and a miracle happens.

Everyone's faith grows stronger, and all rejoice when they hear a first-person account of their loved one's trip to heaven and back again. The theater audience usually cheers and claps at the end of the movie as the credits roll. Everybody walks out inspired and feeling terrific. Me, too.

But what happens when all that you have prayed for doesn't occur? What if there is no return from heaven, and your loved one dies? Family and friends may react to the sudden loss with disbelief, agonizing grief, extreme sadness, depression, and anger.

They may question why God has abandoned them. Their faith may be crushed or, even worse, lost.

I have walked this road. My precious daughter, diagnosed with leukemia, would begin a fight for her life shortly after her eighteenth birthday. As a true believer in Jesus, I felt sure God would heal Jenny. So did she. Why wouldn't he?

With only six words, the doctor delivered a powerful blow that day: "This aggressive leukemia is a killer." He went on to tell us that "35% die within the first thirty days. If Jenny's body does not respond to the chemotherapy, she most likely will not be with us this time next year." You can imagine what was racing through my mind as I witnessed my beautiful daughter receiving a death sentence on what should have been a beautiful winter day.

"Dad, I just don't want you and Mom to be sad. . . because I'm not sad." These are the first words that my eighteen-year-old daughter said to me moments after we left her doctor's office. Jenny had stated very matter-of-factly to me that she was not sad, just a little anxious over receiving chemo. But she knew, whatever the outcome, she was in "God's hands." In the snap of your fingers, the world of this young woman, and that of her family, changed. In that instant she went from being a straight-A student, a pre-med major, and a promising college athlete with softball scholarship offers to a person who would begin a fight for her life. And she accepted it. Jenny, never a person to ask "Why me?" embraced the challenge and attacked it like she did her heavy academic schedule or a formidable softball opponent. I think in that very moment, as she looked at me and said, "Dad, don't be sad," she lifted me up and put me on her shoulders; *her* strength would carry *me* through the darkest time of my life. My little girl was about to show me what life, love, and passion was all about.

Over the next three and a half years, while undergoing extensive chemotherapy, losing her beautiful hair (three times), and undergoing a bone marrow transplant, Jenny (the consummate "type A" personality) completed high school, started college, and became the spokesperson for the Central California Blood Center.

The Blood Center recognized that this attractive and popular high-profile local athlete was just the person they needed to get the word out into the community about the importance of blood donations. She knew she was living proof, and she was passionate about motivating the people in her community by showing them that not only she, but countless other kids, needed their life-saving blood donations in order to survive while they battled their cancer.

When she was barely eighteen, Jenny was asked to speak to a crowd of 800 blood donors. She had never given a speech to a large audience before and was pretty nervous. She wore a long, black dress and a baseball cap to cover her bald head and her latest bout with chemotherapy. Her entire speech was only six words: "Thank you. . . for letting me live." Then she held out her arms as if to embrace all 800 people. There was not a dry eye in the crowd, who all rose to their feet for a standing ovation.

Those simple, yet profound, words helped them understand the important part they played for Jenny and the other kids who could not live without a community of blood donors.

After that, Jenny would give her speech to high schools, colleges, churches, civic groups, and anyone else who would listen. Her passion moved them. Here was this young woman, who put aside her own troubles to show what was important in life and how to love thy neighbor—all while knowing she was going to die.

At the time of her diagnosis, I was an executive with a large, national mortgage-banking firm, far removed from the knowledge of what blood, platelets, transfusions, and transplants were all about. When faced with life and death decisions, you tend to become an expert—fast.

Watching Jenny's passion for helping others like her made me get excited about her new mission in life. Now, looking back, I think her attitude and joy in the midst of her trial helped me in my own grief. As a parent, when your daughter is given a death sentence—even if you are hopeful—subconsciously you begin to grieve from the moment you hear the news. It is not a conscious thing that you can point to; it merely takes up residence in your mind and soul and is your constant companion.

It is natural for a parent to worry, but through my daughter, I was able to see what real faith looks like, a faith that continues to pray for healing but rests in the assurance that her illness was not in vain, that she truly was called to be used for a greater purpose. As a result, I began to question what role I was to play in this journey; as a father I felt completely helpless. I could not protect my daughter from this danger in her life. I could only stand by and see what the doctors, and God, would do.

As the months went by, she would have small victories and then relapse after relapse until a bone marrow transplant was her last hope for a cure. There was only a small chance of success, but it was worth trying. Even then, her faith never waivered.

She continued to have a big, beautiful smile on her face and was ready for the fight. Unfortunately, barely two months after transplant, she relapsed once again. This is where Jennifer made a decision that would affect all of our lives.

Once again, it was six words. "I don't want any more chemo." She decided that she would not take any more chemotherapy. As her dad, I had to trust her decision. She explained to me that she still wanted God to heal her, but if He didn't and He had other plans for her life, then she would be okay with that, and opted for quality of life vs. quantity of life.

Jenny continued to attend college taking up to twenty units a semester and getting her professors to waive general education requirements so that she could take upper division courses. Her reasoning? Her time was now limited, and if she was going to die, then she "wanted to die smart!" She said this with a smile, a chuckle, and a twinkle in her eye, but you could tell she was serious. Thankfully, they bought into her reasoning, and she continued taking classes until three days before her death. And still with that trademark smile.

Jennifer continued her promotion of the blood center. Her passion for getting the message out moved a city. This young girl who had thrilled them on the softball field, had won their hearts with her determination and faith to help others, was now about to lose her four-year battle with leukemia. She was slipping away. Her spirit was willing, but her body was yielding to the disease she had courageously stared down.

Jenny was at Fresno State taking classes on Oct. 25th when she began to feel too ill to continue. I was out of town on business at the time, and my wife, Claudia, called me to come home. It would take me until 3:00 a.m. on the 26th to arrive, and Jenny was waiting for me to help her make some decisions.

After much prayer, we decided that she needed to be in the hospital for what appeared to be the conclusion of her earthly journey, so off we went. Once there, the wonderful staff made sure she was comfortable. She received blood, pain medication, and the news from her doctor that she was in her final stage and that she should share with those she loved her thoughts and feelings. Her maturity astounded me as she lay open her heart and soul to her mother and me. What a blessing for a parent to see the fruit blossom in the brief, but well-lived life of their daughter!

A committed Christian, Jenny had so much promise and loved to serve. She knew the Lord had used her mightily in her life's work. So it was a shock when after four years of chemotherapy, hundreds of blood transfusions, and a bone marrow transplant, Jenny lost her battle.

But she didn't lose her miracle! And neither did I nor my wife or the dozens of friends and family gathered in her room the night she died. What we witnessed was the next chapter of a life well lived, a life so pleasing to God that in the midst of her struggle, He would grace her with His presence in her final moments before ushering her peacefully into His loving arms for all eternity.

I'm sure different people could interpret Jenny's musings in many other ways, but we who witnessed the exchange truly believe that Jenny was speaking with Jesus. At that moment He had opened her spiritual eyes—a loving moment with her heavenly Father in which He was showing her His beautiful glory and that she need not be afraid. And she wasn't. Her faith had been rewarded, and He was welcoming her into His presence. In doing so, He had blessed all of us in that room with the honor of seeing her lovingly speak with Him as He revealed His glory to her.

For those few minutes, calm occupied her room as we waited for her final breath. I was stroking her left arm with my left hand, my right hand cupped under the back of her neck, keeping it straight as she lay in a semi-comatose state. Her daddy, so close to her in life, holding her one last time. The end was very close.

I cannot explain what happened next except to say God wanted to give sight to our faith and reveal to us the beauty of a believer coming home to Him.

Jenny, who had been too weak to move or speak for hours, suddenly sat up in bed, opened her eyes, looked to the heavens, and said, "Jesus" in a clear voice when she recognized Him. Then she laid back down, eyes closed. A few minutes later, as I continued to hold her, she asked, "Where's Mom? Tell her to come join the celebration!"

Claudia came alongside as Jenny, with her eyes still closed, declared, "Mom, the celebration," as if there was a wonderful party going on!

Finally, Jenny sat straight up one more time as if looking at Jesus face to face and lovingly said, "Oh Lord God, Your glory is over all the heavens and the Earth."

Those words would be her last.

I looked at Jenny as she lay back, and I saw such peace. I leaned across her to whisper in her right ear, "Jenny, Daddy loves you, and it is okay to go be with Jesus." I kissed her one last time. Jenny took six more breaths and was gone.

A spontaneous chorus of the old hymn "How Great Thou Art" rang out, signaling her departure. An aunt said later, "This was the happiest sad day ever." I praised God for allowing us to witness this home-going. As a father, I take much comfort in knowing where my little girl is.

A miracle? Maybe not the one we desired, but a miracle nonetheless.

God showed us a glimpse of what awaits us. Jenny's life was short, but she willingly led us to a deeper understanding of what happens when we breathe our last breath on Earth and, at the same moment, take our first breath of glorious, heavenly air.

I certainly rejoice with all those parents who get their children back who then live long and productive lives. I also rejoice knowing Jenny fulfilled her heavenly Father's assignment on Earth.

Claudia and I grieved like all parents grieve. . . intense and heartbreaking and almost unbearable. . . but with one difference. We knew, without a doubt, that Jenny was safe, happy, and pain free. We also knew, because of our own faith, that one day we will both join her.

Our faith also has been rewarded. My daughter's mission was over, and mine had just begun with the promise that I would carry on her work. To me, it was like I received a spiritual transfusion. In facing death, my teenage daughter discovered her purpose in life—and helped me rediscover mine.

Two days after she died, I stepped in to speak on her behalf about blood donation and haven't stopped since. I started out as a volunteer and have now served as the President and CEO of the Central California Blood Center since 1999.

My daughter has led the way in the work I now dedicate my life to as a result of the promise I made to her, and she has shown me the context that I should put my grief in. There is no need to grieve for her; I grieve only because I miss her and the wonderful relationship we experienced. I can accept that while longing for the day I see her again. If Jenny is happy, so I must be.

I can live with that. Now that is a miracle!

Dean Eller spent twenty-nine years in executive management positions with national mortgage banking and real estate firms. Fulfilling a promise he made to Jenny the night she died, he carried on her passion for blood donation. Dean became CEO of the Central California Blood Center in 1999. For more info, or to donate blood, please visit: www.donateblood.org. He can be reached at: deller@donateblood.org

....

CHAPTER TWO

POWER OF FORGIVENESS

A Journey to Forgiveness
By Dianne Rogers

My defining moment, unfortunately, was a mother's worst nightmare. However, when recalling those events, I believe they brought me a deeper understanding and greater connection to God.

Had tragedy not struck my family, my first defining moment probably would have been the birth of my two beautiful sons. Although they were born two years apart and shared a number of similarities, they were dramatically different. Chris, the oldest, was handsome, had brown hair, brown eyes, and the darker complexion of my French ancestry. Sean was beautiful with his white blonde hair, blue eyes, and a lighter complexion favoring the Irish side of our family tree.

When Sean was born, he looked like a little angel. However, his angelic appearance had no influence on his rambunctious nature. One of his favorite pastimes was roughhousing with his brother, climbing up, down, and over anything that did not move.

Both boys loved playing frequently with their beloved cousins, as ours is a close-knit family. Chris was, by nature, the more studious of the two, and began reading very early. He independently joined the Jacques Cousteau Society when he was five years old. Although I was separated from their father, Tom, life was moving along, and I adored my little family. However, soon a chain of events was set into motion that would change my life forever.

Returning home from work late one evening, I was in a horrific automobile accident. I felt death all around me, yet, somehow, I had escaped it. My recovery, however, was painfully slow and dealing with two very active youngsters was difficult, even with help. As time went on, my physical strength did not return quickly, and my emotional state proved to be fragile as well.

Not being able to go back to work, money issues were mounting, and the stress of not knowing when I could return to work was a daily grind. My doctor suggested I get away for a week of rest.

I took his advice, and a friend and I went to Lake Tahoe in Northern California to camp on the Truckee River. My spiritual connection to nature made it a good choice as my body and heart needed healing. I arranged for my boys to stay with a trusted friend who had been their occasional babysitter. While gone, I called at night to check on the boys and to tell them I loved them. At the time, Chris was six and Sean was four.

It was five days later, and I was camping in the heart of a forest. That beautiful, crisp October morning, I awoke to the aroma of coffee brewing. It was late in the season, and the campground was empty except for my Volkswagen camper.

Around 7:30 that morning, with my day just beginning, I peeked out the window of the van. I could see the sun streaming through the trees, falling to the ground and shedding light upon the birds scratching for their breakfast in the newly-fallen snow. I felt at peace for the first time in a long time and warm, despite the freezing cold outside.

Still sleepy, I heard a voice in the distance calling, "Mommy." It was a little voice, sounding confused and lost. It gave me chills, but I thought it was the cold air as I got out of the camper and asked my friend where the child was. I asked if he had heard the child calling, "Mommy." He said, "no". . .we were the only campers there. I told him it sounded just like Sean's voice. By now, I had been gone five days and was missing them more than ever.

I decided when I called them later that night I would tell them I was coming home early. When I called that evening, I was caught off guard when a stranger answered the phone, advising me to call my parents. It was just after 7:00 p.m. when I quickly placed that call.

My father answered the phone, at first hesitant, so after a few words I asked to speak with my mother. He said she was sleeping, and he didn't want to wake her.

My mother and I enjoyed a very close relationship, and she would have wanted to speak with me even if it meant waking her. The conversation became oddly strained as I asked about the boys, but my father kept interrupting, asking when I was returning home. Something in his voice was very alarming as he suggested I fly home that evening. I told him that was impossible as there had been a snowstorm and the only airport in town was closed. I asked him again about the boys, and he said everything was fine and we would talk later, abruptly ending the call.

In my heart, I knew something was terribly wrong. I just didn't know how terrible or how wrong it would be.

Having ended the call so quickly, I called him back and the line was busy. Nothing was making sense. I called the boys' father, Tom, and his line was also busy. When I did finally reach him, his words were tentative and his voice strained. I asked what was going on, where were the boys, and then he told me Chris was with him, but that Sean had been in an accident earlier in the day and was in the hospital.

My mind was racing with questions. He, too, suggested I fly home immediately. It was then I realized everyone else was talking, just not to me. Frustrated, I hung up the phone to find my own answers. There were only three area hospitals so I called each one, explaining that my son had been admitted under emergency conditions, and I needed to talk to the nurse in charge. Each hospital I called said the same thing—there wasn't any patient admitted with that name.

With each call, my hysteria and fear grew. It was now almost 10:00 p.m. and my last phone call to Tom would soon reveal the reason.

I asked where he had been. He said he had gone to the hospital to check on Sean. I told him he was lying, saying I had called all the hospitals and Sean wasn't in any of them. He kept telling me I was wrong, that Sean was in the hospital.

Finally, in desperation, I yelled, "Tommy, he's my son. I don't care how bad it is. I want to know where he is so I can talk to him."

I repeated myself several times, each time my voice rising in fear and anger. The eventual answer was a parent's worst nightmare.

After a very long and confusing pause he replied, "He's dead. Sean's dead."

As if the defiance in his voice could alter the terrible truth of his words.

I remember screaming and calling him a liar. My voice rising and falling in panic and confusion, asking why he was doing this to me, screaming at God, and the four walls that tried to contain me.

Finally, when the truth of his words could no longer be denied, my knees buckled and I fell to the floor, unable to move, unable to think, unable to be. I remember the phone ringing, and others in the room talking first with my father and then with my doctor in San Diego. As I lay there, I dissolved into nothingness on that shag carpet. I was taken to the area hospital and given heavy sedation and extra medication for the long ride home.

I don't remember leaving the hospital. I just remember waking up in a crowded parking lot and seeing the rooftops of cars encrusted with ice from the newly-fallen snow. And over those, a flashing neon sign, in much need of repair, recommending the "best breakfast in town."

I was led from the van into the sharply-lit restaurant; a cup of coffee had been placed before me. I couldn't understand why I was so groggy, and then the realization hit again that my precious Sean was dead. My body caved into the cracked and peeling plastic seat of the booth where I sat. Now sobbing uncontrollably, I quickly fled to the van and the journey home.

I slept the entire way until we turned the corner to the street where my parents lived. I looked out the curtained window of the van. I saw family members waiting for me in the driveway and on the stairs to the porch. All I could see was my son Chris standing in front of my Mother, her hands on his small shoulders. Shoulders I unknowingly placed a burden on each time I told him to watch his brother. . . because he was older. An admonition I could never take back.

Chris was all I could see, all I wanted to see. I was numb with disbelief as I got out of the van. One by one, speechless family members came to embrace me, their tear-stained faces lined their own pain. All I could do was put both hands up in protest saying I just needed to see Chris. I knew if I allowed myself the luxury of those embraces I would disappear forever into a black hole of grief. I had to try to be strong for Chris.

When I made my way to where he was standing, I knelt down in front of him and he said in a small little voice, "Mommy, Sean got hurt. Can we go see him?" Wrapping my arms around him I said, "I know he did, baby, but Mommy is here now." It was later that day when his father, Tom, and I explained that Sean was now in Heaven with God. Even now, these words open wounds that never quite heal, and I weep remembering the sorrow of those days.

As the details of the accident unfolded, I learned how it happened. . . or as much as I could bear to hear. Half-truths, I suppose, for fear of giving too many details. It was early in the morning; the boys were outside on the patio playing with suction darts and German Shepherd puppies. Leaning against a stucco wall was a large, stringed mechanism framed in wood, once a piece of a larger musical instrument.

The boys were playing with that dart game and soon after, it was placed atop the frame against the wall. Later, when Sean saw the darts, he decided to climb up and get them. Chris, sensing the danger, repeatedly told him to get down, but Sean did not heed his brother's warning of danger. Sean climbed to the top and, while pulling on the strings, he pulled the frame over and it fell down on top of him. It killed him instantly as Chris witnessed the death of his little brother.

The irony of strings did not escape me as my little angel entered the heavenly realm; I believe it was Sean's voice I heard that morning at the campground, calling, "Mommy."

That first day home, the house was full of people, coming and going, offering condolences, bringing food and flowers, stories and tears. But I felt hollow, with nothing to share but exhaustion and wanting to disappear. The last thing I remember about that day was lying across the bed in my parents' guestroom and hearing what I thought was the distant wailing of a wounded animal. Finally falling asleep, I realized the wailing came from me, my own pain-filled cries going out into the night.

When Sean died, the entire family structure became broken. Aunts, uncles and cousins, grandparents, his father, his brother and I—all broken as it was not the natural order of things. Parents should outlive their children, not bury them, but such was not to be the case for us. Sean's death was the first of three, as two of my sisters lost their sons to accidents, too. They joined me in a club no one wants to be a member of—the price of admittance too high and painful.

As much as everyone assured me that it was not my fault, feelings of anguish, grief, and guilt were constant as I believed his death was somehow my fault. If only I had stayed home, nothing would have happened to him. Those days turned into months, and with each one's passing, I found new reasons to blame myself for the tragedy that had befallen my family. My world became a constant litany of "what if" and "if only" and angry conversations with God.

In those early days, loving family and friends surrounded me, but soon everyone returned to their normal lives and routines. Although I lived close to my family, I felt alone in my grief and overwhelmed by my circumstances: a mother with a young son who needed me more than ever. I failed him often, consumed by my own emotions.

The guilt I felt each time I looked at the pain in Chris's eyes sometimes kept me away from him; it became too much for me to bear. The strength of his aunt and uncle and his grandparents kept him wrapped in love as I tried to make sense of the senseless. My days were long and the nights longer as I lay crying and hoping for sleep that would not come. I knew nothing of what lay ahead for us. I only knew I could not endure even one more day with the burden of guilt and the heaviness of grief surrounding Sean's death.

On a day I thought could be my last, I went to a small church where I would often go to light candles for Sean and pray for forgiveness and at times even try to barter with God. Inside there was a beautiful inner chapel where the nuns would celebrate mass with a side room where they would go to pray in private.

I remember that day as if it were yesterday. I had taken Chris to school, after which my aimless driving brought me to the nun's front door again. I entered the chapel, and, to the left, was a smaller room containing a life-sized statue of Michelangelo's Pieta, the Virgin Mary holding the lifeless body of her son, Jesus, after He was taken down from the cross.

Entering that intimate space, the presence of Their likeness was overwhelming. Feeling unworthy, small and alone, I sat in the back of the room with my head down, sobbing, yet daring to look up, feeling so drawn to the Mother who, too, had lost her son, I went to kneel directly in front of her. Her pain so evident and yet her face so beautiful, expressing a serene sweetness and acceptance of what had befallen her beloved Son. I felt my pain mingle with hers as she tenderly held her son, knowing I could never hold mine again.

As I knelt before Her, heartache permeating my entire being, the weight of its burden was never heavier as horrible thoughts raced through my mind. In anguish, I cried out, "Oh dear God, please help me!" I was afraid to think of what I might do—to myself, to Chris, to us both. I had never been more afraid in my life.

All those months I had prayed and prayed, but this was the first time I had spoken those words aloud, perhaps feeling a last resort, now openly pleading for His help. Choking on my own tears, I looked up into Mary's face once again. In those next moments, I felt a gentle calmness surround me, washing over me as a wave of unconditional love. In those moments, I heard His answer when He said:

"Be with me now in this moment and know that you are loved and all grace shall follow thee. Be not afraid for I am all and everlasting. Go now and be at peace."

For the first time in almost a year, I could feel and see light in what had become the end of my tunnel. My tears still flowed but seemed more of relief than despair, as they washed away some of what I had carried with me for so long. Leaving the chapel that day, I felt a sense of hope, that one day I might be able to forgive myself.

Over the years, I have stumbled and fallen many times, and I have been my own worst enemy in some things. However, God's Grace saved me that day and, remembering that, I try to be kinder to myself, knowing that He thought my life was worth sparing. I alone could decide how to face it: Grace or bitterness.

In sharing this intimate time in our lives, I hope you can see that things do get better. It's very hard to do at times, but give yourself permission to laugh, to eat, and to love, for the child you are grieving is still with you. You have only to recall them; they can no longer touch you with their hands, but they can always touch you with their hearts.

My beloved son, Chris, survived this tragedy; however, the pain of the moment still lingers. His way was not easy as he struggled to make sense of it all, feeling, too, that somehow he was to blame. Now a grown man, I am so proud of him. He is a loving son, married to a wonderful woman, and a man his little brother would be very proud to look up to. His father, Tom, remarried and has two other sons whom Chris is close to. As a family, we endured this painful time in our lives as it lashed us together, and for that, I am very grateful.

Losing a child, in my opinion, is the worst thing that can happen to a parent. It is not something we ever get over, but with time the pain is less sharp and allows the good memories back in. I can never know what our lives would have been like had Sean lived, but I have come to the understanding that the will of God knows what the soul needs.

I am so grateful we had Sean with us as long as we did, and I praise the day both of my boys were born. I am also blessed to have five wonderful step-daughters who fill my life with light and love. Being a parent is the most honorable job I could have. I didn't always do it well, but I try to be the mother that all my children can take pride in.

What I want to say here is this: there is hope after the death of a child, as impossible as that might seem. However, we must be free to talk about our loss, unafraid in the face of it, as we try to find our way back to reason.

Please do not isolate yourselves; find strength in family, friends, and God. When Sean died, there was no grief counselor, no therapy groups; that aloneness left me feeling apart from the whole for too many years. The old saying about strength in numbers holds true, even in this.

Surround yourself with people who love you and reach out to those who have shared your pain. The road can be rough, but we need not travel it alone.

As I knelt before the Pieta that day so long ago, asking God for His help, I still hear His words.

"Be with me now in this moment and know that you are loved and all grace shall follow thee. Be not afraid for I am all and everlasting. Go now and be at peace."

Dianne Rogers is a writer and lives in Southern California on a horse ranch with her architect husband, Will. She can be reached at: diannemrogers@gmail.com

To Forgive, Not Forget
By Martha Tessmer

"Hurry, something bad has happened," repeated the frantic voice screaming through the telephone. In a scrambled state of mind, I shifted from late night sleep to panic as my husband and I jumped from our bed into the car, rushing to the intersection we'd been told to report to.

Turning the first corner, our breathing quickened as we saw the neighborhood orchard lit up in the darkness as though daybreak had come early. Rounding the second corner brought into view emergency vehicles, a crashed car, and two ambulances—one pulling away.

With the door still open on the second ambulance, I saw a large body and a small body lying inside. As we approached, an officer stepped forward and put to words what we feared, "Donovan didn't make it."

Involuntarily, my screams came in reply. The person who later shared the agony of hearing me being told, "Your child is dead," turned out to be the smaller body in the ambulance, the driver of the car—Donovan's girlfriend.

"Not my son. Please not my boy," would plague her repeatedly. For me, my mind was haunted with a vision of the yellow tarp spread over my precious child. The cause of the crash that took Donovan's life involved distracted and reckless driving. No one in the car had been drinking or doing drugs, and the driver was not texting. Rather, the music was blasting; they were laughing and joking around with each other and the three backseat passengers were wrestling over an energy drink and bag of chips. To get a better wrestle going on, they did not put on their seat belts.

The passengers started teasing the driver to go faster to add to the fun. She caved into the peer pressure, drove recklessly at an excessively high speed, and lost control of the car. When the car hit the first tree, it bounced off and the back door flew open. As it did a reverse spin, the unbelted backseat passengers were ejected; Donovan died upon impact. The car crashed into a second tree, pinning the driver inside.

When released from the crash site and granted permission to move forward in a direction of our choosing, we knew immediately which road we were to follow. Some have referred to it as the high road. We simply knew it was the right road.

"We know Donovan is in Heaven now. But we need to go to the hospital and check on the other kids from the car. Above all else, we need to be the one who speaks with the driver first to remind her we loved her when she left our home, and we love her still. We forgive her." The words rolled off my tongue without hesitation.

As the hospital elevator doors opened, we stepped out. My eyes scanned the faces of neighbors and friends while my mind struggled to register the unfamiliar location, the hospital waiting room—such a stark contrast to the high school football field where we normally gathered to watch Donovan lead his team. Blank stares, creased foreheads, and wet cheeks bore witness to the tortured hearts of these familiar friends.

The room went silent as my family stepped into the waiting area. Gasps confirmed they had not expected us to join the vigil of those awaiting updates on the other passengers. I asked the person nearest me, "Where are the other kids? How are they doing?" Donovan's friend explained three were in the Emergency Room, and one of the boys also ejected from the car was in surgery.

We stepped toward the parents of the young man whose life was in the hands of surgeons. No words were needed. They stood, we embraced, and my voice rose up in prayer.

Shortly after, a social worker entered the waiting room and reported the teen had been placed in a medication-induced coma in hopes his broken body would recover. As the woman started to retreat, I tapped her shoulder and introduced myself as Donovan's mom. Only one question needed an immediate answer, and it came quickly, "Where is the driver?"

I explained my family's desire to speak with her. Whereas I expected a reaction of surprise, I did not expect the intensity of her indignation. She burrowed her eyebrows in a scowl and with conviction insisted we could not see the driver. After a few unsuccessful exchanges, my next words were emphatic: "In this moment we have a child's life in our hands. What are you going to do? We want to speak with the young girl, offering her our love and forgiveness—to help, not harm her. Don't make me get on my knees in front of these people and beg."

Surprised at our repeated request, her response came as a single word, "Fine." She turned. We followed and waited in the hallway while she went into the Quiet Room to speak with the parents now separated from anyone involved in the crash. Even though she tried to dissuade them with warnings, the parents asked her to let us in.

When they shared with their daughter our offer of forgiveness, the girl became more unstable. Meaning Donovan's girlfriend no further harm, we left, having delivered our message. In departing, though, we offered to return when their daughter felt up to a visit. The call came the next day as my family left the mortuary. In keeping our promise, we rallied our broken spirits and headed towards the hospital.

Upon entering the Intensive Care Unit we saw her broken body connected to the ropes and pulleys helping with physical healing. The young girl's face contorted with emotional and physical pain, emerging as endless tears coupled with a sobbing apology, "I'm sorry. I'm sorry." She looked at us with desperate pleading, "I'm sorry. I'm sorry."

My husband, daughter, and I approached together, each step bringing us closer to crossing the line of simply believing to actually living out mercy and faith—no hesitation, no doubt, no second guessing about what we had come to offer. We gathered around the bed, one by one hugging her while she continued to weep uncontrollably. When my turn came, I took the young girl into my arms and turned my head to find myself staring into the framed picture of my son positioned at the foot of her bed. As I stared into the eyes of the child I could no longer hold, I held this child and whispered, "You can tell us you're sorry today, but forgiveness means you never have to say those words to us again." It is then that words became actions as we delivered forgiveness to Donovan's friend. We focused on our feeling of wanting no harm to come to this girl. Whereas our journey was just beginning, we knew hers was as well.

The paths we traveled were at times shared or parallel and other times a solo trek. Present or not, our hearts remained connected with love unwavering. When she faced the potential of four years of imprisonment, we fought for her freedom. At each court hearing my whispers to her became, "This does not define you."

In time, God's plan for our forgiveness and her freedom materialized. The defining moment for all involved in the crash came with the decision to let a national non-profit film Donovan's story. Not one of the four teens hesitated to tell of the last moments shared and reckless decisions made the night my son's legacy became lessons to learn from his death. Everyone set aside their own discomfort for the sake of helping others.

Equipped with the video and passion to save lives, I shared a national platform with law enforcement officers—and spoke to millions. My strength comes from God; my resilience from knowing each heart touched allowed Donovan to make a difference from Heaven above.

Helping others thrive motivates me as an educator, speaker, and author. Through my spoken and written words, I pray God uses the lessons endured to shed light on the value of life and the importance of protecting it.

Martha Tessmer lives in Central California and continues to travel and speak about the dangers of distracted driving and teen safety. To book Martha as a speaker at your school, church, or community, please visit: www.1voice2hear.org or email: martha@1voice2hear.org

Molly Day
By Doug Griffin

> *"When a child loses his parent, they are called an orphan. When a spouse loses her or his partner, they are called a widow or widower. When parents lose their child, there isn't a word to describe them."*—Ronald Reagan

How do you tell a story of your greatest challenge and God working through your pain rather in spite of it? For me, it has to begin with a child.

Grace

"She's in a better place." Such words meant to console a grieving parent over a child who has died are brutally unfeeling or cruelly ignorant, wouldn't you agree? Ironically, you might say, these words were shared with me, but by someone in the perfect setting and with the perfect name. The speaker was Grace, an eight-year-old who spoke these words to me at my first time back teaching Sunday School after the worst experience of my life. I had lost my beautiful, twenty-three-year-old daughter to a drunk driver. Oh, the power of a child—a recurring theme in my life that started with my Molly.

Now, after losing Molly, I might have been tempted to think, "Why would you take Molly after all I've done to serve You?" God does, after all, frequently intervene in human affairs. Our prayers are often answered in the affirmative, albeit not with the timing that we would prefer. Yet some prayers are not. So why not protect Molly? Why not have the car in the turn lane next to her start to pull out? Why not prompt Molly so she saw the truck coming before she pulled out on the green? Or why not prompt the drunk driver to have taken evasive action, or why not just cause mechanical difficulties with the truck, or have his friend, who also died that night, stop him from driving in the first place? Why not have a cop out on the road of infamous speeders on a Saturday night? Why, why, why?

Of course, this also begs one more "why" question: why did I deserve the twenty-three years, five months, and twenty-six days I had Molly? I know the answer to that one: I didn't. That was all about grace, too.

In the late 1980s, I had nearly blown up our marriage just three years in with a one-year-old son at home. I had what might charitably be described as an early mid-life crisis upon turning thirty. I think a huge moral failure would be more accurate. Fortunately for me, God intervened. My wife, Doris, displaying an incredible strength of character and loyalty, stuck with me and we reconciled. After a six-month separation, I found myself back home and in marital counseling. Our family survived. And thirty years of marriage later, we're still a home.

After we reconciled, I was going through law school when we found out Doris was pregnant again. And so, on a beautiful, sunny San Jose morning in August of 1991, I heard the words from the doctor that steered my life into the sweetest direction it had ever been aimed: "We have us a girl person." For Doris and me, Molly was God's reward for having stuck it out when splitting would have been so easy.

Finding God for Real

At this point in my life I must honestly admit that God had mainly been only a passing concern for me. I had grown up going to church as a check-the-box activity on Sundays, only to be ignored the rest of the week. After having kids, Doris and I had begun going to church because something inside of us knew that we should. Children have a way of doing that. Which brings me back to Molly...

With the softening of my heart and through circumstances I can only conclude were somehow prearranged, I soon rededicated my life to Christ; I was on my way. Now, as my life at church began to take shape, I was almost like a kid again, soaking things up like a sponge. I savored what the pastor would teach and joined a men's group. Another pastor encouraged my attempts at serving.

I then did any number of things at church. I was a greeter. I acted in dramas we used to do. I became a trustee. I led a men's group. I went to leadership conferences. Heck, I even coached the co-ed softball team on Friday nights. But what captured my heart, prepared in advance through my Molly, was the day in 1999 when I walked into a classroom to try working with kids. I quickly saw that this was for me. And what became instantly evident and what I can never fully explain is why and how God put an amazing love for children in me that I never really knew existed. And did it ever take off.

Soon I developed a passion for both teaching and evangelism. The main reason I knew God was in this for me was the passion I brought to it week after week and how He would give me words and insights while I was teaching that I had not even prepared to say. And these were usually much more powerful than the text of the lessons that were prepared. In the now eighteen years I have had in front of children, I have easily been used to lead more than a thousand children to faith in Christ.

I became the volunteer director of our grade school ministry for a couple of years while budgets were tight. I started a more intensive discipleship program called DNA for kids interested in taking their faith to a higher level. And it all started with a little girl who had my heart at home.

Fortunately for me, while Molly was in high school, God used this love for children as a catalyst for something more: he placed it in my heart to adopt a little girl from China. And in what can only be attributed to God's intervention, within nine months of the time we went to our first adoption meeting, Doris, Molly, and I were in China, adopting our Paige. So I had another little girl in my life.

A few years later, Molly, having been an incredibly successful student through high school and college, was now working as a nurse at Madera Community Hospital. She combined her serious intellect with a drive to succeed and topped it off by being very shrewd. The time had finally come for her to move out on her own, and she was buying a house.

And then the weekend of February 20, 2015, came along.

The Worst of All Worsts

The day before the accident was a Friday, and I faced some pressure at a board meeting. As I spent time in the early hours of Friday morning in prayer, I quieted my mind after a serious time of asking for help and guidance—for business. I then heard the following words in my mind, "Just remember, I love your children as much as you do." I am not one to claim to hear words from the Almighty, but I had heard this phrase at least once before. However, in this context I had no concept of what it could mean. Forty-eight hours later, I would find out.

When we got the call from Molly's friend Emily's mother at 5 a.m. or so Sunday morning, we immediately panicked. The police had just rousted her out of bed—Emily was in the ER as a result of a car accident. Eventually we had our greatest fears confirmed—Molly had died. And it wasn't just an accident; it was a drunk driver.

As word spread and people starting showing up at our house, it came rather quickly to me that I had to forgive the driver, even before knowing any details. I wish I could say that by my willpower and through some courageous act I made this decision. But that would be a lie.

This time, perspective came quickly, calling through the Holy Spirit. "Do you not remember driving as a young man while intoxicated yourself? Did you not come within an eyelash of dying in a car accident yourself when you were twenty-two? Are you not commanded to forgive in order to be forgiven? And what is it that you hate more than anything? Hypocrisy."

While this may seem like a process, it was actually a very quick realization. So quick, that by the time the first reporter showed up at our house, the first words out of my mouth were these: "I just want you to know that we have forgiven the driver." As the reporter struggled to pick her jaw up off the floor, I continued, "You see, we are Christians, and we are commanded to forgive. Did you know that Jesus forgave the very men who murdered him from the cross? If he can do that, I can forgive the driver." I must also confess that I didn't want to be known as the angry father who screamed for retribution or revenge. But this was not about what I wanted—it was about what I was compelled to do.

I do also want to note a hero in this tale. When the accident occurred, another car had been at the intersection with two brothers. The only reason they had not pulled out, and were not the ones hit, was that they were having a disagreement over something. After the accident happened, the young man driving that car called 911 and stayed with my daughter and with Emily, who was critically injured, until help arrived. For Molly, it was too late, but young Reggie stayed with her and held her hand as God took her home.

So, how to go on? How to stand into this unceasing grief? Fortunately for me, perspective fueled by the Holy Spirit came calling again. I told Doris that we needed to celebrate Molly's life on her birthday and not focus on how she died. I said we needed to have an annual Molly Day. Doris, with a little help from her friends, took my idea and put it on steroids. She turned it into #livelikeMolly and came up with the perfect way to honor her: perform acts of kindness for others to establish her legacy as the kind, loving, wonderful person she was.

It turns out my friends in the media, not to mention all our friends at work, church, and in the community, thought Molly Day was a great idea. It took off all over our hometown, reaching into other states, and even into Canada and England. No substitute for losing our child, but at least God could use it for good.

The story might have ended there, but one final chapter remained: the sentencing of the young driver. In California, the judges are required to let anyone speak who was impacted by a crime. While Doris and I each struggled with what we would say, we were not quite prepared for what would happen in the courtroom.

What I never saw coming was that the three speakers before us, Molly's friend Katie, Emily's mom, Kathy, and Emily herself who barely survived the accident and was still in rehab, each expressed their sorrow and their pain . . .and their forgiveness.

As Doris struggled through her remarks, I felt such a sense of pride in her. Never a public speaker, her words and her attitude were perfect. And she, too, expressed her forgiveness.

As I then rose to speak, I fought through the tears; I shared with the drunk driver what I was sure Molly would say: "You took my life, you nearly killed my friends, and you hurt every person I ever loved. . . and I forgive you." I also admonished the young man to do something great for God with his life, that God had spared him for a reason and he needed to figure out what that was.

Finally, our story and Molly's has hardly ended. Dozens of people have shared with me the power of our testimony of forgiveness and of Molly Day. It is my hope that some will give Jesus another look after seeing what He could do through us in the midst of this tragedy. This August 26 will be the next Molly Day. As the years go on, I can only hope that Molly's legacy will carry on even beyond my lifetime, and our pain will continue to be used for God's goodness.

#LiveLikeMolly

Additional Resources:
Facebook: #LiveLikeMolly
Twitter: #LiveLikeMolly
www.CompassionateFriends.org—a nonprofit for bereaved parents and siblings.

http://www.avid-advocatesforvictimsofimpaireddriving.org
AVIDD—Advocates for Victims of Impaired Driving Support Group. Drinking and driving is a choice, not a mistake.

Doug Griffin lives in Fresno, California with his wife, Doris, and their daughter, Paige. Their son, Joe, lives in Hawaii and is a proud member of the United States Navy. Doris works as an administrator at a community college. Doug is still a practicing attorney. Doug can be reached via email: dgriffin@californiabf.org

Two Angels, One Life
By Melanie Warner

"How many children do you have?"

I often struggle with how to answer that question while not sucking all of the energy out of the room. I've learned to say, "Five. Three here and two up there" as I point upward toward Heaven.

Early on in our marriage, my husband and I had a miscarriage with our first child. We had been so excited to have a baby, yet it was so early stage, we didn't even get to know the sex of the baby. We deeply mourned the loss of our first child, but continued to move forward. A few years later, we had a beautiful daughter and named her Kyla.

Our second child, Cole, came a few years later. The pregnancy and the birth were fairly easy without any complications.

A few years after Cole was born, I was pregnant with our third child, Carson. He was perfect and healthy in every way. Our doctor suggested that we schedule his birth a week early since he was going to be leaving for vacation the following week. Sadly, that turned out to be a fatal decision.

Carson died in my arms. That certainly was not the plan as we arrived for a normal birth at the hospital on August 31, 2005. Through a series of misguided medical events, my uterus ruptured during delivery. Five major arteries lead into the uterus, so it was also life threatening to me. My first thought was for them to simply take it out. I hadn't planned on having any other kids, so Carson was my last one. I didn't know that he was in trouble. The doctor made a fateful decision that day to rebuild my uterus, in spite of the rupture.

The cause of Carson's death was due to multiple medical errors at the hospital during a routine delivery. As it turned out, the hospital had broken over twenty state protocols in their care that day. They had also administered more than eight times the legal dosage of a drug that they did not disclose they were giving to me. It was administered by an unsupervised trainee in the middle of a shift change.

I felt the effects immediately in my body. I struggled with two main questions: was this divine intervention or human error? Why did this happen? I concluded that had I been at any other hospital, Carson would be alive.

When they told me that my baby had lost oxygen and had irreversible brain damage, surviving only with breathing tubes and machines, I began to pray for Carson. God had, after all, saved my life; surely he could also save Carson if I prayed hard enough.

Unfortunately, the swelling in Carson's brain became worse, and he slipped into a coma. All of his organs had shut down, and he was only surviving with machines. After a few days, we had to make the horrific choice to take him off of life support.

I wrestled with this decision as I continued to pray, feeling that if we made the decision to take him off life support, somehow we were giving up on a miracle. Then I understood that he could have just as easily died alone in the hospital. I was grateful to be able to hold him, surrounded by family, and experience one of the most difficult, yet spiritual and beautiful moments of my life, one that changed me forever. We should all be so lucky to die surrounded by loving family like that.

That was when I realized that I had other choices about coping and grief. I could choose to sue the hospital, go through years of litigation, reliving these horrific moments over and over again—all of which would not bring Carson back. I could choose to be angry with the people who were responsible for his death, but they were the same people who also saved my life. It just felt wrong to sue the people who had saved my life, even if they had mistakenly killed my son. I had to drive by that hospital every day. Did I want to carry that anger with me daily?

I chose forgiveness. I chose to look for gratitude in everything. I did not want to live with anger or feeling like I was a victim. That decision to forgive gave me instant peace and calmed my spirit.

At first I couldn't understand why our prayers for Carson to live and be totally healed seemed to go unanswered. As time went by, I slowly began to understand the miracles, blessing, and gifts that had come from Carson's life and even his death.

Doctors told me that my son had saved my life. His position in my body had kept my organs intact. Had I continued to push during labor, I would have bled to death in under a minute. I was devastated, but proud that his brief life had a purpose in saving mine. I also struggled emotionally with guilt because a mother's job is to give life to her children—not children sacrificing their own lives for their mother.

In the days that followed, nurses from the hospital called to tell me how special Carson was and that he had touched their lives forever. They watched him rally and fight for his life, in spite of his circumstances. One doctor came to me in tears telling me that this experience had changed the way he thought about his own life and children.

Another doctor told me that my faith and positive attitude during this trauma, and the fact that I lived through this, had motivated him to rethink his own belief system. Friends, ex-employees, and even family members who had not spoken in years because of anger or arguments were suddenly coming forward and forgiving the past. People I knew who had suffered from drinking problems or drug problems said that Carson had inspired them to change their choices in life and given them the courage to stop. Some prayers that had been prayed for over thirty years were suddenly answered as many people transformed in days.

My husband and I struggled emotionally with this tragedy and had to explain to our other two children why their brother would not be coming home. It broke my heart each time our four-year-old son, Cole, asked, "Am I still a big brother?" My daughter, Kyla, was eight when this happened. She softened the blow for all of us when she said, "We thought we were getting a little brother, but we got an angel instead. What could be better than that?" She was proud of her brother, not sad like the rest of us. Many times she would get frustrated with our grief and say, "He's in Heaven. Isn't that a good thing? Why are you so sad?"

It's unfortunate that it takes a tragedy to bring people together. It's a sad part of human nature. Just days before Carson's birth, I was consumed with issues like employees, clients, laundry, traffic, bills, children not cleaning their room, and many other things that felt like major problems—things that stressed me out, made me irritated or angry.

I wasted so much energy on these things. I realized that I was living my life as if I were some kind of victim of all of these circumstances. Now I realize that I made myself a victim by taking so many small issues and making them large. Now I'm no longer a victim; I'm a survivor, and there is a *big* difference. I will no longer take for granted my health, my life, my family, my friends, my company, my wonderful and capable employees, the sunset, or anything else that seems like "daily life." The small stuff should never be taken seriously as big stuff.

Before this experience, I used to pride myself on working a hundred hours per week; I defined myself by what I did for a living. I recalled looking out the window early in my career, thinking "someday I'm gonna own this town." Now here I was looking out the window of a hospital, narrowly surviving something that most women did not. I sadly realized how long it had been since I had simply slowed down to gaze out a window. All I could think of was, "someday, I'm gonna serve this town."

Then another miracle happened. We wanted so much to have another child. After a ruptured uterus, most doctors deemed it was unsafe to have another child. So we thought about adoption and even considered a surrogate. For years, we tried to come up with ways to add to our family, but we hit a wall at every turn.

Finally, I surrendered the situation to God and gave thanks for the two healthy and amazing kids that we had. I donated all of my maternity clothes and all of Carson's baby items to a local women's shelter.

Three weeks later, I found out I was pregnant! My husband was very nervous and did not think it was safe. But I knew that this was God reminding me that he had not forgotten about me.

I found a very rare doctor who had successfully delivered babies after a ruptured uterus. Nearly three years to the day that Carson was born, Hudson, our little miracle man, came into the world.

I believe that because of the choice of forgiveness, God rewarded me with another son—a miracle baby. He was healthy, and we had no complications. If the doctor had not made the decision to rebuild my uterus, I would have never had that option.

If Carson had lived, Hudson would not be here today. Now I see Carson's purpose in Hudson's life as well. It felt like a small redemption that the doctors were able to give me another son. It certainly didn't replace Carson, but was an answered prayer for me.

I felt the need to share my story because I want people to understand not to fear their death, but to live their life. Hope and joy can still follow deep tragedy. I know now that God shared such a private moment with me to prepare my heart for the death of my son. I now understand that Carson is the lucky one. He is in a great place, and I can't wait to get there. Most importantly, my son does not need me, but my family, my other kids, and my community *do* need me.

Through the series of miracles and seeing how his life has touched so many others, I now have the gift of feeling pride and joy when I think of my son in Heaven—not sadness.

I hope by sharing my personal experience with people that they think of their own lives. Don't wait for a tragedy to remind you of what is really important in life. Go out and mend a broken relationship, let go of anger toward someone, enjoy the sunset, get to know someone better, appreciate the little things in your life, live without regrets, and most importantly, connect with people.

My greatest hope is to see people taking care of themselves and each other. The hardest part for me to swallow was that this death could have been prevented and was caused by mistakes at the hospital. I am not angry or bitter. I chose to forgive the people who made these mistakes. We did not sue them. Instead, we lobbied for changes at the hospital. I'm proud to say that this same hospital has made major improvements that have helped save many other lives, even so many years later.

A few months ago, I was sitting at dinner with a group of people and a man at the table next to me introduced himself as a new doctor in town. He told me he was at that hospital because of me. I didn't know that Carson's story had become famous in the medical community, or that it had become a landmark case in California that had instigated changes in protocol at many hospitals and even instigated changes to the information and brochures of the medication by manufacturers.

Now, the law in most states requires women to sign off before they are administered any medication during labor. That factor alone has helped save countless lives of other women and children. It might never have happened if we had simply sued and walked away with a little bit of money.

I chose not to live my life in vain (or my son's). I feel that I am now able to help other people who are in pain. I have never been angry with God and have tried to find the good in all of this. Finding things to be grateful for, in spite of tragedy, was the key to my own healing.

We honor Carson every year on his birthday and Christmas by buying presents for what age he would be. We then donate these gifts to our local Children's Hospital where he lived most of his life here on Earth. Now when we buy balloons, we don't keep them until the air comes out: we keep them for one day, then we let them go. We say that we are sending the balloon to Carson in Heaven. Another way we honor him is by living our lives to the fullest and remembering that no day is promised.

After I lost Carson, I started seeing how things tied together. It was easier to connect the dots. I stopped focusing on the reason he died. I stopped asking "why" as there was never a good answer. I realized it was a selfish question that only held me back. Once I stopped looking for the reason why my son died, I truly learned the purpose of his life and my own.

I started asking other questions. What can I learn from this situation? How can I grow from it? How can I help others who are going through it? Where does my life go now?

Slowly, God began to reveal the answers to those questions. Through that process, I started reaching out to other parents who had lost a child. It gave me comfort to hear their stories and how they had also survived it. It gave me hope. That hope and healing led to the creation of the book you are now reading.

I also started a local Compassionate Friends chapter in my hometown. This is a wonderful organization for parents and surviving siblings to come together and offer support to each other during the critical coping process.

None of us know what we can do until we have to. We don't choose for our children to be hurt, or sick, or killed. All we can choose is how we respond to it. How we choose to live our lives in honor of them. It's not a switch that can be turned on and off externally by others. We can't allow our entire lives to be defined by these brief or horrific moments. They are only seconds that could change our lives forever if we choose to allow them to. Defining moments can also come from joy.

We are all in this human thing together, and some of us handle it better than others. If we can somehow help others through their dark times, it gives us purpose—something to live for and look forward to.

> **Melanie Warner** is a magazine publisher, speaker, and author who lives in Fresno, CA with her three children, Kyla, Cole, and Hudson. She is the founder of the Defining Moments book series. To submit a story, or discover additional books, visit: www.mydefiningmoments.com or email her at: Melanie@ mydefiningmoments.com. You can also submit and follow stories on Facebook: My Defining Moments

Just One Life
By Violeta Astilean

If there is anything worse than losing a child, it is losing a child to a drug overdose, because grief is accompanied by judgment and blame. It's the most gut-wrenching, helpless feeling to watch your child suffer at their own hand, from their own decisions.

What is different about losing a child to overdose? Losing a child to addiction means you didn't get to say goodbye, and you have to deal every day with the stigma of being a parent whose child died from drug use (if you are brave enough to be truthful about the cause of death).

You question your every decision. You look for what you did wrong, what you didn't say, why you didn't have a second sense that something was wrong. You look back over the years, dissecting each part of their life, looking for clues. And you look at yourself and ask all of the what-ifs.

You look for blame, but mostly you blame yourself. You find an online group of mothers just like you, where there is no stigma and everyone has the same questions and feels the same pain with no judgment. You force yourself to read the coroner's and toxicology report hoping there is an answer there. And you cry—a lot.

I lost my son, Theo, when he was twenty-five years old to a fatal combination of heroin and Fentanyl. That might be the one thing others remember about him, but I remember him as a warm, open, loving, bright, intelligent, and very handsome man. He had a huge laugh and a fabulous smile.

He was an outstanding athlete, with many trophies and awards. He played football and was a linebacker—that was the brightest shining star in his life. He was also very gifted intellectually, being an honor roll student in high school, and then dropping out of college after his first year.

Theo was a fun-loving, free-spirited, beautiful son with a heart of gold and a contagious smile. He had a tattoo on his wrist that read, "Just One Life." He lived his life with wild abandon, no regrets.

Theo always had a way to make you smile and laugh as he had a wonderful sense of humor. He was charismatic; wherever he went, he never knew a stranger. He always made you feel welcome. He was a gifted storyteller and always an entertainer. He loved his little brothers with all his heart. He was a loyal friend to many.

He always said, "I love you, Mom. I am sorry, Mom. . ."

We were very, very close. Even during those horrible years of drug use, he and I never became distant from each other. It was torturous at times, but the one thing that was always, always apparent was that he loved his family and his family loved him— no matter what.

Theo started smoking pot in the last years of high school. His drug use progressed into pills and then cocaine. We believe his addiction started several years prior to his death, but it's hard to say for certain because this disease of the devil entered our home slowly and quietly.

Over the next seven years, he experimented with a variety of drugs, including his final drug of choice, opiates. During those years, Theo tried so hard to stop. He felt broken and guilty for the hurt he inflicted on his little brothers and me. He once wrote about his "fairytale life" that he had screwed up so badly, and his self-esteem was completely eroded towards the end. But he always took total responsibility for what he did.

Theo was such a fun-loving individual, though he had his own inner struggles. The difference between Theo and most other kids when they were in the process of getting help was that Theo reached out for help entirely on his own. He loved his friends and family so much that when his behavior started to hurt the ones he loved the most, he decided it was time to do something about it. He asked for help and entered a rehab program. He was clean for about seven months when he relapsed.

September 30, 2014, was the first time that my son called me, crying and asking me for help. It was the first time he admitted he was a drug addict. In my shock and heartbreak, I didn't criticize him for it because I knew he felt so bad. I knew he felt he had let us down. He didn't want to be an addict. He told me he hated that life, and he didn't want to live that life anymore. "Mom, please help me," he said. "I will do anything to get out from this hole." The first step to recovery is admitting you have a problem, so that was a good sign.

He shared why he decided to go down such a dark path, how alone he felt although he had so much love from me and so many people growing up. How it all started with just having a little fun with pot at seventeen with his friends and escalated to prescription pills and cocaine. The hardest part of being a parent is watching your child go through something really tough and not being able to fix it for them.

My son was in a detox program for thirty days. Afterwards, we sent him into a treatment center where he was kicked out after four months—for using Facebook. We sent him right away into a halfway house thinking he was ready. After three months there, he relapsed again. Then he tried a sober living facility, but ended up getting kicked out. After one week on the street, my son was found dead from an overdose. He died alone in a motel room.

FBI and DEA research shows that about 46,000 people die from drug abuse annually in the U.S. That is more than the number of Americans who are killed in car accidents and gun violence combined. Half of those drug-related deaths are from opiate drug abuse.

The numbers are appalling and shocking. Tens of thousands of Americans will die this year from drug-related deaths; more than half of these deaths are from heroin and prescription opioid overdoses. Opioid abusers have traveled a remarkably dangerous and self-destructive path.

This epidemic does not discriminate. Addiction can happen to anyone. All across this country, it is taking good people from good homes, even honor roll students and star athletes, and leading them down a trail that often ends in pain and sadness.

For me, the pressure and fear of watching my child battle addiction was like a roller coaster with good periods and crashes. You learn to be hyper-vigilant, living always with fear. You have hope as well. As long as they are alive, you have hope. But the sound of the phone ringing at night or not hearing from them in a normal way makes your heart sink. It's always in the back of your mind that your child could die in some way as a result of their addiction.

I never imagined my son would die. He sought treatment on his own. He was motivated and really wanted help. He cared about his family. He tried to make the right choices. I heard about so many kids dying, but I always said to myself, "No, not my son. He will be okay. He will recover. He will come home after recovery, and life will be beautiful for my family again."

The fateful day arrived on May 17, 2015. There will never come a day, hour, minute, or second that I stop loving or thinking about my son. Child loss is a loss like no other.

Theo was an incredibly loved young man. Friends flew across the country to be at his funeral, and expressions of incredible sadness about how his death could have been prevented just permeated the air. Because of the shame he felt, he never asked his friends for help.

To the kids reading this story, you are loved and have so much to give to the world. The temptation to abuse any kinds of drugs is very real, but the courage to resist that temptation is also very real. When people do drugs, it affects the people around them more than themselves. If my son's story saves even one life, then his life and death were not in vain.

My advice to parents is to read and become informed as much as they possibly can about addictive illness and drug use from responsible sources early on. Talk honestly about the risk factors of becoming addicted by "experimenting." Talk about family history of alcohol or substance abuse. Start talking early to your kids about the dead end of drugs, even legal ones. In our experience, tolerating marijuana led to many other dangerous substances.

Recovery exists; recovery is possible, you just have to believe it and help them as much as you can. Addicts need your support and love. Show them you love them, no matter what. It's a long road. It's a hard and exhaustive road, but it's possible.

Tough love doesn't have to exist. Like any other human being, people with addiction must be treated with dignity, care, and respect.

As I grieve his loss, I expose myself to the risk of having sorrow, frustration, anger, and guilt. When my son relapsed for the first time, I was shocked. I felt so scared and disappointed. What should I do now?

I knew he was smoking marijuana and thought it was fairly harmless. In no way did I think it would escalate to cocaine and, ultimately, heroin. Many prescriptions cost a lot more than heroin you can get off the street. I regret that I did not intervene sooner when I first learned my son was smoking marijuana. At that time, when I complained to some people about my son's actions, their response was, "It's okay; everybody's smoking marijuana. It's even legal now."

We don't know who is going to develop an addictive personality. It could be any one of us. Theo was bright, funny, and so very intelligent. He wasn't at all what you might think of when you hear the word "addict." I would like to advise all parents to start talking about drug abuse and the consequences with their kids from an early age and don't underestimate marijuana as a gateway drug to other substances.

The empty space of my missing son lasts a lifetime. I will miss him forever. There is no glue for my broken heart, no elixir for my pain, no going back in time. For as long as I breathe, I will grieve and ache and love my son with all my heart and soul. Being his mom is the best gift I've ever been given.

Even death can't take that away.

The message is everywhere. Be happy. Don't take anything for granted; seize the moment. Live life to its fullest. We all have. . . just one life.

Theo Marinescu
10/7/1989—5/17/2015

Violeta Astilean lives in East Hampton, New York with her husband and two sons, Alex and Max. She plans to start the Theo Marinescu Foundation—Just One Life—for education, awareness, and rehabilitation scholarships to help people suffering from drug addiction, working closely with schools to develop training and education, inspire knowledge and inform change by educating and advocating to prevent and reduce deaths and tragedies. She can be reached via email at: violeta11937@aol.com

CHAPTER THREE

ANGEL BABIES

Seeds of Hope
By Cookie Bakke

With the proliferation of the Internet, who has not seen the picture of the tiny hand reaching out of an incision in a womb and clutching the finger of the surgeon performing a miracle en utero procedure to enable the baby's live birth three months later?

Ultrasound technology has zoomed forward from the white dots of the '60s that estimated only fetal weight to what we view today. Doctors evaluate and repair the tiniest of heart valves while parents watch in awe, able to see details as small as eyelashes. With these advances come not only the ability to determine the sex, but also to see if the baby has Dad's big nose or Mom's little nose. There's a person in there, a son or daughter, a baby with a name and identity. And when the unthinkable occurs, the pain of loss can be immeasurable.

My own story began with those ultrasonic white dots. Pre-RhoGam, my AB-negative body had become allergic to positive blood. They call it Rh isoimmunization; it translated to my body, identifying the fetal blood cells as a virus and then ridding itself of the offenders. The result was fetal demise before outside-the-womb viability.

As the world was stunned by the earliest heart transplant (December, 1967), another radical medical procedure was being developed to enable a different kind of miracle. Intra-uterine-transfusion was, by today's standards, barbaric, but when introduced, it lowered the 100% death rate to 80%. The mother's body fought harder to kill invading red blood cells. Medical science, with the help of donor cells, fought harder to save babies. As technology marched ahead, so did the success percentages.

The U.S. programs, initially five carried out in teaching hospitals, were experimental. As the first person in the world to have two live births enabled by IUTs, it was frightening to again find myself pregnant years later. A titre is the measurement of antibody levels—and mine were high. Still, abortion was out of the question for me, so it was back to the examination table, the improved ultrasound capabilities, and the world of needles, needles, and more needles.

This time there was an additional complication: a frontal placenta that blocked access. To go through the placenta was a very real threat to mother and child. Internal bleeding was a probability because the placenta contains a tangle of internal vein/artery growth—and that kind of bleeding would result in two dead bodies. There was only one small area that would permit entry in my case, but how can anybody line up the exact right place on an inside baby with the exact right place on the outside mother?

It worked once, but each IUT can only get in a limited number of red cells before the baby experiences cardiac distress and the procedure must be halted. When we tried again, "Ben" was thoroughly uncooperative. His head would be on the needed place, or his spine, or his heart; he assumed every position except the one we needed. As an inpatient, we did an ultrasound almost every day. I tried lying on my back, my side, nearly upside down; with every try, I caught glimpses of a child who was defying all odds of survival.

So many children fight valiant "outside" battles; this little boy fought that battle from inside.

A C-section was scheduled for a Tuesday, and the neonatal team was readying to do battle outside. On Saturday, however, I just felt funky. Based on "mothers just know," it was ultrasound time. Ben was too quiet. The ultrasound showed nothing unusual and no edema (which would have been a bad sign) was present. To my delight, the doctor suggested I go have a high calorie lunch and then come back for a second peek. I downed a cheeseburger, fries, and a Coke, then got back on that all-too-familiar examination table.

Sometime in that hour, the "almost made it" little heart had ceased to beat.

The C-section to terminate the pregnancy was performed the next morning. At a healthy and expected weight, he looked perfect. But there was no breath, no cry, no life. His battle had ended, but medical science got a slight boost at the well-charted inside experience of this little warrior.

Even though I had walked in knowing that the odds of a live birth were astronomically against his survival, the death came as a tremendous blow. It felt as senseless as a drowning or a car accident. The most difficult part for me was trying to conquer the anger that seeped into the grieving process. Somehow I mixed up the "how could I do this to you" with "how could you do this to me" and realized with something beyond distress and self-loathing that I was somehow compensating by being angry with a baby who made the finals of a billion to one fight.

To this very day, I vividly recall the process of clawing my way out of that intense grief. I gave myself little time to wander in my thoughts and instead decided to learn everything that I could about hematology, immunology and every other "ology" I could find. Yes, it filled the empty space—as did immersion in hobbies and events that enriched the lives of my surviving older children. However, in looking back I now understand that time is what gives us the ability to heal, and acceptance is the accommodation we employ to understand the true meaning of "it is what it is."

What it is. . . is a journey. Every step along the way creates a foundation for a ripple of change. Somewhere out there in this big, wide, learning world of ours is a later-born person—in Ben's case many persons—who beat their own odds because of the knowledge gained by each and every earlier case.

Grieving is an experience. Experience is what teaches us, and time is what allows us to recognize experience. I now know that there are wrong things to say to one who grieves. "I know just how you feel" needs to be locked into every human being's voicebox and never allowed to escape. Nobody knew how I felt. Hearing those words elicited what was almost a rage. When something unspeakable happens to anyone around me, the only words, at least to me, are, "I'm here." Better yet, just a silent hug.

I also know that we are all different. For a long time, I did not understand when a woman would weep uncontrollably at a miscarriage during the first trimester of a pregnancy. After all, I'd lost a perfectly formed and assumed viable infant, so what was a collection of cells the size of a thimble? In that experience was yet another lesson.

Grief at the loss of life is privately suffered. There is no one-size-fits-all experience.

One might think that this ends my story. Surprisingly, it doesn't.

When Ben died before he lived and I was wheeled into surgery, I opted to not sign the tubal ligation papers. The presumptuous insanity of that decision is absolutely worthy of questioning. I have no idea, even today, why I was not willing to sign. It just "was what it was."

Six years later, after changing my name to "Grandma" (because that's what I was by then), actively joining corporate

America with a career change, and having survived getting all of my children into their twenties, I got the ultimate surprise. My own reasoning that a gastrointestinal malady I had assumed was from drinking unboiled tea on a night train into Shanghai—after all, none of my "lady parts" were working—was a nine and a half week pregnancy. What?

On the positive side, medical technology had somewhat advanced. On the negative side, I was in my mid forties. I was a serum donor because my titers were so high, and the immune system repercussions for sixteen prior transfusions made my body an unspeakable battleground. Abortion, even at billion to almost none odds, was out. No one, anywhere, had ever had three IUT babies survive. My tiny sliver of hope came from wondering if "the grand scheme of things" might connect, somehow, some way, somewhere.

Twenty-four weeks later, Kimberly Evana made her own piece of history by checking into this world at four pounds and three ounces after a rollercoaster ride between life and death. Her Apgar score was one. In the first twenty-four hours, she had a double exchange transfusion (thanks to her uncle being on site with cross-matching blood) and went into seizures. There were tubes in every part of her body. On day two she opted to spit up the ventilator and, as neonatologists rushed to get another in place, they stopped short because she was breathing on her own.

Having lost 80% of her red cells en utero, suffering cardiac failure, and her venous system shutting down at twenty weeks gestation was part of that wild ride, but like her almost older brother, she just kept fighting. I had my own fight going on. Was I equipped to be able to care for a child who might predictably be brain-damaged because of lack of oxygen-carrying cells? Would her other organs be intact? Would the seizures have damaged her even more? There were more questions than answers. Once again, acceptance was key. "It is what it is."

Yes, my baby-birthing days are over. I am sixty-eight years old, and Kimmi is now twenty-four years old. Not only did she defy all odds, she surpassed all expectations. Prior to her fourth birthday, the local television station came out to "interview" her. It happened to coincide with George Washington's birthday.

"Kimmi, do you know who George Washington was?" She replied, "Yes, he chopped down a cherry tree." The announcer then asked her if Washington was as smart as she was. "Nah, he didn't know nuthin'," she answered.

So why did a TV station want to interview a three-year-old? Because she had recently become the youngest member of Mensa in the western United States with a 99.6 percentile IQ score. The worrying was needless. And to the fortune-telling gypsy who randomly stopped me one day, pointed at my young blonde miracle, and imparted the cryptic message, "There is a reason she is here against all expectation. One day she will change the world," I send a "thank you"— an affirmation that all is right in our world.

The big picture of these many years has helped me accept the ultimate learning. Life has a way of evening out. In the face of untold and unimaginable adversity or loss lives the seed of hope. To the extent that you may grieve, so shall you also celebrate— another time, in another form.

Whatever the mode of appearance, what will be *will* be.

Cookie Bakke is a high energy "polymorphic." She's a journalist, enrichment lecturer for multiple cruise lines, licensed private investigator, advocate for victims of fraud or major crimes, consultant, author (*123 Main Street… the Scamming of America*), columnist, global fraud expert, volunteer, logophile, travel afficionado. . . and, in her most important roles, a mother, grandmother, sister, aunt, cousin, best friend, and lifetime partner. She can be reached via email: johncookefr@gmail.com

Incompatible With Life
By Shari Savage

Motherhood never interested me until I got pregnant, at which time I took up the flag like a zealot. When my three children were 3 ½, 2, and 3 months, it was clear to me that baby Madeleine needed a partner; two pair seemed right to me in every way. After six miscarriages and a few related near-death experiences, I was no stranger to gestational calamity, and my doctor advised (rather harshly, I thought) against any more pregnancies. Ever the optimist, I was convinced that number ten would be the perfect, safe, disaster-free finale. At age forty-two, I sailed into my routine amniocentesis with few worries.

The call came at night, after the doctor's office was closed. It's some kind of sick ambush at a time when you can't do anything to respond. I was changing Maddie's diaper when the phone rang, and my world turned upside down. "Birth defect, incompatible with life," said an emotionless voice on the other end. Incompatible with life? They must use that ridiculous term to make sure it doesn't sink in until after the call is over. Whatever they pay the person who has to make those calls, it isn't enough.

Stunned and disoriented, I told my husband. He didn't grasp the concept any better, and we fell to our knees. I'd love to say we stayed there, but when you have three in diapers, anything that's not in flames or actively bleeding has to wait. Later, on my knees again, I complained bitterly and selfishly to God about what I wasn't getting out of the deal—no happy pregnancy, no "two pair," not even the joy of picking the baby's name. Clearly and distinctly, a voice said, "Her name is Christiane Rose." Not a voice in my head or in my heart—a voice in the room, completely present. I knew in that moment that whatever was to come, God would be there with us. I got off my knees and calmly told my stricken husband that the baby was a girl and that her name was Christiane Rose.

In this kind of crisis, as in most others, people self-sort into two categories: those who desert you and those who don't. And forevermore, you'll remember them exactly that way. The lesson came quickly: my obstetrician's office informed us the very next day that unless I was coming in to discuss "terminating the pregnancy," I would not be able to continue as a patient. Two more days, two more obstetricians, both unwilling to provide prenatal care for a baby who, as one so eloquently put it, "is going to die anyway." Finally, a nurse ran interference for us, and we were gifted with a wonderful obstetrician who wanted only one thing: the opportunity to have ongoing conversations with us about our experience so that he could understand our perspective in order to be a better doctor.

I was grateful that my beliefs did not make abortion an option for me. It's a terrible choice, and I don't judge those who have to make it. I knew that even though we couldn't see it at the time, there was joy in there somewhere; we needed only the patience to let it unfold. Ending the pregnancy would not sidestep the grief, but it would eliminate the possibility of joy.

We told almost no one. I loved everything about being pregnant and didn't want to be robbed of my happiness by sad faces and sympathetic tears; there would be plenty of time for that after Christiane's death.

We passed the next few months in a disjointed mix of expectation, anticipation, and consuming grief. Our generous doctor insisted that we have a thirty-minute ultrasound every two weeks, which he personally administered. This was our time to be with Christiane—to watch her grow and to delight in her as she sucked her thumb and grabbed her toes.

When there is not going to be anything after the pregnancy, your definition of lifespan changes: this was Christy's life, and those ultrasounds were our time to be her parents. We looked forward to each one, knowing the only memories we would have were being made in those precious minutes.

Our grief was so intense, and we were often buried so deep inside it that we sometimes couldn't console each other. We recognized and respected that, leaning on one another when we could and giving each other space when we didn't have anything else to give.

I took walks in the rain so that I could cry openly without anyone seeing. My neighbors probably thought I was crazy for walking without an umbrella, but it helped. I also called friends and relatives who lived far away. They let me rant and make the selfish complaints I couldn't make to anyone around me. For all I know, they just put down the phone and walked away during my tirades, but it helped and I'm grateful.

I learned quickly that there is a hidden network of support for parents experiencing perinatal loss: the special team of nurses who assemble to deliver children who won't survive; the seamstress who custom-made Christy's tiny going-away gown to my precise specifications and then refused to accept payment; the funeral home who handles the arrangements for newborns at no charge; the church people who executed her service precisely as I had planned it (and in those months of waiting, I had plenty of time to plan).

When your life walks down the street and turns the corner without you, when you lose not only the present but an entire future, every moment is precious, every detail critical. For the rest of my life, I'll remember every person who was so kind.

Too quickly, the day after Madeleine's first birthday, Christiane's time came. My other labors had been stunningly rapid—all under an hour—but I could not bear to think of Maddie growing up with the day after her birthday being the day her sister died.

With seven hours to go until midnight, I asked God to please give me one last gift—more time. At 9 p.m. the doctor informed my husband that our baby was dead; I was hemorrhaging, and if we didn't deliver her soon, I would bleed to death. We agreed to the Pitocin injection and prepared to see our baby.

The gift came: the baby waited, and just minutes after midnight, we welcomed Christiane Rose. We had been educated about her overwhelming physical defects, but nothing prepared us for the shock of seeing her for the first time. God had one last gift in store for us, however, for the moment we laid eyes on her, our hearts were completely flooded with love. We held her, talked to her, and loved her for a long time before the final goodbye. I wouldn't trade those moments for anything, and my heart breaks for those who never experience them.

I must have been a sight at the funeral—walking up the crowded aisle, two babies in my arms and my son, then four, walking bravely beside us. My husband spoke to the full church. His words were touching, the raw grief of a father. I delivered a message about our journey and God's love.

In being Christiane's mom, I learned a few things.

The first was that the purpose of our life is to serve God, and that limiting our definition of life limits our definition of service. Christy never drew a breath, and yet she filled the church on a weekday morning, mostly with people who didn't attend church and who heard a message of redemption and hope. By my definition, she lived a full life.

The second was that we are a self-centered lot, egoistic by nature, and we tend to believe that everything that affects us is about us. Christy's drama wasn't about me, or my husband, or anyone else. We were just bystanders, and our only job was to behave in as responsible a manner as we could, doing no further harm.

Third, you're still the parent, and you have the right to make decisions for your child. This experience is a blunt lesson about how much is totally out of your control so making whatever decisions you can, no matter how small, reaffirms your parenthood. Assert your authority: you'll feel better.

Finally, I learned that in our lives of unprecedented comfort, most of us have very little opportunity to reach deep inside and discover what we're really made of. I knew I was tough, but in loving and accommodating Christiane, I learned that I'm also very kind, I can be patient, and I can sacrifice without reservation for someone else's benefit. In short, Christiane taught me to be a good mother.

When Christy was born and died, I felt like a marathon runner. It wasn't important to have won the race; I ran well and was proud to have crossed the finish line with integrity, happy to have done my best.

Christiane Rose would be eighteen now, a high school senior, and I think of her every day. She looked like Maddie, who sometimes feels the inexplicable loss of her counterpart. I miss the experiences I didn't get to have with her—missing front teeth, the first bicycle—and the experiences I'm not going to have, like prom, graduation, and college. Just the same, my heart is at peace, knowing I did the very best I could.

> **Shari Savage** is a freelance business writer and personal biographer. She lives quietly on a small lake in West Michigan with her husband, Harry, and their rambunctious goldendoodle. She can be reached at sharisavage2@gmail.com

The Grief Letter
By Jill Hammond Jackson

I was adopted as a kid, so all I had ever wanted was my own family that I could call my own. I wanted to make sure my adopted parents always loved me, so I strived to be the best at everything I did. I got straight A's. I was a star athlete. I met and married the man of my dreams, John, and we had a beautiful baby girl. We named her Chelyn Sue after my sister.

She was a cherished baby and gave me so much joy. As a new parent, I often questioned myself and wondered if I was doing everything right. I was adjusting to learning how to be a mom and it often left me feeling anxious.

One sunny afternoon, I put my daughter down for a nap. She was six months old. When I went back to get her, she was blue. It was ruled as sudden infant death syndrome (SIDS). I was shocked, as I couldn't believe that she was gone so suddenly. The hardest part was the guilt that I felt as a parent, like somehow it was my fault. I felt like I had done something wrong.

I never really recovered and was afraid of having any other kids or going through that type of pain again. I had a hard time feeling anything after that. I felt numb and shoved my feelings down inside. I told myself the biggest lie of all: "I'm fine." In a sense, I buried my daughter and myself. My family wasn't sure how to handle my grief or talk about it. Did they call me on Mother's Day or not? Should they call me on Chelyn's birthday or not? They didn't want to remind me of the grief.

I buried myself in work and really just shut down for a long time. My husband was my saving grace. He and his friends cleaned out her room and supported my emotions. I couldn't even walk into her room without bursting into tears. He was my angel and my best friend. I don't know what I would have done without him.

Later that same year, my husband was out of town working on a bridge. He was an experienced ironworker and loved his job. I walked in my house and the phone was ringing. I assumed it was John. Instead, it was one of his co-workers. He told me that John had fallen ninety-five feet and had died instantly. I was in shock. I couldn't even process it.

After the funeral, I was alone with my grief and went into a dark place. I had buried my entire family a few months apart. My daughter and my husband were dead. I just couldn't process that the two people I loved the most in the world were gone. I felt hollow.

How did I handle it? Not well. I locked myself in a hotel room and drank heavily for several days. I even cut off my beautiful long hair that John loved so much. I was so angry at him for leaving me.

Looking back, it sounds crazy. But at that time, it was just my way of grieving. It wasn't healthy. I would say to anyone else who is dealing with great loss: embrace the grief, do not ignore it. If you numb yourself, it changes you. I couldn't feel anything for a long time. Allow yourself to grieve.

Seek counseling. Do not swallow your grief. At one point, my mom came outside and saw me crying in my backyard. She wanted so much to help me feel better, but there was nothing she could do. She said, "Where is Jill?" and I answered, "She doesn't live in here anymore." She said, "We miss you, Jill. We want you back. Is there anything I can do to make it easier?" I told her there was nothing anyone could do to make me feel better. At this point, it was ten years later, and I was still empty and grieving. My grief had become my family.

I decided to go to a place called Progress House to face my grief for the first time. I lived there for three months. There were many other people there who were going through something heavy in their lives as well. It helped to hear their stories and realize that some were even worse off than I was. Somehow, it made me feel better about my situation.

Part of my process was writing a grief letter. I wrote one letter to each of them, as if I were talking to my daughter and my husband, like they were in the same room. In the letter, I said everything that I wanted to say to them. I was angry that they left me. I felt alone and had been holding it in for so long. I apologized to my daughter for not protecting her. I told them I loved them and missed them, and that I thought about them all the time. When I wrote the letter, it was my way of processing all the loss; I never expected a response.

Soon after I left the Progress House, I took a trip to Italy to clear my head and continue to heal. It was something that my heart wanted and needed. I was walking up the Spanish Steps in Rome when a young man, who was asking for change, stopped me. He said, "I really need to talk to you." It caught me off guard. This complete stranger was so urgent as he looked me straight in the eye and said, "I have something to tell you. Your husband and your child want you to know that they are okay, and you will be okay." I stood there, blinking in the sun, staring at him, trying to register what he was telling me. How could he have possibly known my story? I often wonder. . . if I hadn't gone to Italy, would they have found a way to get that message to me through someone else?

After that, I felt like angels were walking with me. I knew that my husband and my daughter were with me. It was the first time I had smiled in years. I wish that someone had told me to write the grief letters years ago. I finally was able to let go of all the emotions I had buried inside. It was so revealing and one of the most profound things in my life. I learned that it's okay to feel sad because at least it means I learned how to feel again. Since that time, I've been able to feel again, and even find love again.

Jill Hammond Jackson lives in Madera, California with Jerry, her husband of 17 years. She can be reached via email: mizzjilly@icloud.com

Three Days
By Jennifer Davis

There I was—leaving my hospital room three days after Juliet was born. Sitting in a wheelchair getting ready to go home, my lap was piled high with flowers, stuffed animals, and congratulatory notes. It was topped with literature on "How to

Cope," "Losing a Child," and the few garments she wore during
her short life. As my husband wheeled me down the new mom
corridor for the last time, I saw beautiful balloons, smiling faces,
and looks of joy as mothers held their babies. I felt sad and
ashamed that I couldn't share their joy. . . if only they knew the
pain of leaving the hospital with empty arms. The last thing we
did before we left the parking lot was to release a balloon to the
sky. Somehow it felt right, almost like sending a gift to her.

Juliet's birth and subsequent death were more than nine
years ago, though it feels like yesterday. That being said, it does
get easier with time. It seems so cliché to say that, but it has rung
true for me. The first week was unbearable. The first month was
awful. The first year was painful. The second year was like a dull
ache. Now in the sixth year, I think of her often and am okay. I
feel like I've made peace with what has happened, though there
are definitely still twinges of longing.

That January day was a special one for me because I was
twenty-nine weeks pregnant and so excited about going to get a
prenatal massage. That morning, though, I started having mild
cramps. I didn't think too much of it because a friend of mine had
had major pains when her ligaments were stretched, so I chalked
it up to that. I wasn't due to go to my OB/GYN for a few more
days, but once the cramps continued, I started keeping track of
them. I called my husband and when I started reading the times
to him (intervals of five to eight minutes apart), he suggested I
go see the doctor to get checked out. I went; the nurse checked
me out (I wasn't dilated), hooked me up to a machine that
measures contractions (nothing showed up), listened to the baby's
heartbeat, and told me that all was well and that they'd see me
next week for my normal appointment.

Thinking that I must just be a wuss for complaining about
these "cramps," I decided that my massage was just the thing
I needed to relax. I have to say, I really enjoyed my massage.
While I was getting it, the cramps did slow down. The minute I

got home, though, they started again. I tried to relax. When the pain worsened, my husband suggested that we get to the hospital to get checked out. I was a sobbing mess; I knew that something was wrong.

Once at the hospital, I checked in and implored the woman at the front desk that I needed to see someone ASAP. That seemed to fall on deaf ears. Since my water hadn't broken, no one seemed especially concerned. No contractions were showing up and Juliet's heartbeat was fine. Once they finally measured me, I was eight centimeters dilated, and the doctor decided that I was too far along to stop my labor. I guess my pain was warranted after all.

Before I knew it, I was wheeled into emergency surgery. While I couldn't see what was happening, I knew once they had pulled her out of my uterus and I didn't hear any crying that something was terribly wrong. It wasn't until weeks later that my husband recounted the events to me from his perspective. When they took her out, she was blue. They gave her CPR for more than five minutes before the neonatologist, who must have been asleep or in a different wing of the hospital, came sprinting into the room and took over the chest compressions.

At some point they whisked her away to the NICU. I never got to hold her. Considering that she was pretty far along in gestation, however, I knew the rate of survival was very good. I wasn't completely panicked. . . only because I didn't know to be concerned.

When I finally got to go to the NICU (more than twelve hours later), I had to be wheeled down because I felt dizzy. When I saw her, she was hooked up to all sorts of machines, had tiny felt sunglasses placed over her eyes, and was behind the plastic casing of the incubator. I couldn't touch her, as they said it would be too stimulating. They did take off the "sunglasses" at one point. Her eyes didn't blink, even though the light was shining right in them. I think I knew then that she wasn't there; those machines were just keeping her alive. I tried to hold out hope.

Over the next three days, it was like a roller coaster—talking to doctors, visiting her in the NICU, seeing friends/family who came to visit, trying to stay positive. Her vital signs would get better and then worsen. I learned to interpret the beeping of the monitor and the strange figures on the screen to know whether she was doing better or worse.

Day two had been a good day; we proudly showed off our new baby to our friends and family. On the evening of day two, things went from bad to worse. Her blood became acidotic, meaning her blood pH was all wrong. This caused her to crash.

The neonatal nurse in the NICU patiently performed chest compressions for nearly an hour trying to get her heartbeat stable, all the while telling us to talk to Juliet and provide her with the stimulae that was previously unwanted. I will never forget Juliet's eyes during that time—open, pupils dilated but blank, staring at nothing. My husband has told me that the night of day two was the darkest of his life. It was even harder on him than what was to come. He told me that he felt guilty for bringing her into a life of pain, which she hadn't asked to be put through, and everything that she had endured during her short life.

When the nurse said the neurologist wanted to meet with us to go over her brain scan, I was worried. My husband and I sat together, right by Juliet's incubator, as the doctor proceeded to tell us that she had brain bleeds in both sides of her brain. One was a three and the other was a four, on a scale of one to four, with four being the worst.

In so many words, she told us that Juliet would never be able to function on her own. I was in shock. She said there was a private room where we could go to talk. My husband and I sat on the couch, hugged, and cried. When he told me that he thought it might be a good idea to take her off of life support, I was broken-hearted and relieved all at the same time.

While I didn't want to lose a child, I also didn't want her (or us) to have to suffer through life. It was an extremely difficult decision, one that still haunts me at times, but which we ultimately believe was the best thing we could do for Juliet. A grief counselor at the hospital suggested that we not tell anyone what really happened, because most people wouldn't understand. So we told all our friends that Juliet died from a brain hemorrhage, which is the truth, albeit incomplete.

In between all the horrible things that happened, there were so many bright spots from people that truly cared for Juliet and us. I'll never forget when an awesome nurse gave us two stuffed socks with faces drawn on them and suggested that my husband and I put them in our shirts so that our smell would get on them. He could then put them in the incubator with Juliet.

That was so touching to me. It still makes me smile to remember those socks in there with her. We still have them, stored away with the blanket she was wrapped in during her last moments alive, which we sealed in an airtight bag to preserve her smell. Somehow, it is these happy memories that made it so difficult—it was the loss of all the potential future moments of happiness that were the hardest to lose.

I remember the first time I went outside of the house after everything. We had been home from the hospital about three days, and Lee suggested we just get out and do something little. We went to Target. We were back in probably about thirty minutes, but it felt like such a big trip. I remember him saying, "You can do this. It's only been a few days, but before you know it, it will have been a week, then a month, then a year, then two years." He was right. That first year was definitely hard, especially getting through all of the firsts. Mother's Day was particularly painful.

I coped by talking. I talked to friends, family, etc. I also found a support group of others who had lost children. While I was reluctant to go at first, I am so glad that I did. It was the only place that I could go where other women truly understood what I was going through. I knew I wasn't going to be judged. I could cry. I could smile. I could be angry. They supported every emotion I had.

I was able to process all of those feelings without bringing every minute detail up to my husband, which was good because it didn't seem to help him to talk about it. It just made him hurt more.

I have to say that I am so proud of the way my husband and I pulled together to support each other during that awful time. We are stronger now because of it. In fact, losing Juliet helped me realize what an amazing husband I have. I can't even begin to describe everything he did (and does) to take care of me. I can't imagine having to watch your spouse go through all of that. Not only was he concerned with losing Juliet, he was concerned about losing me, too.

My relationship with God definitely got a jolt after losing Juliet. While I had never been super-religious, I definitely pulled away from religion afterwards. I was mad at God. I was mad that everyone's prayers didn't work. I was mad that I didn't force the nurse to admit me to the hospital. I was mad in general. While I wouldn't say my relationship with God is a great one now, it is definitely getting better.

In the first few years after Juliet's death, we would release a balloon—just like we did the day that we left the hospital. Now we just remember and talk about those three days, some of the most impactful of our lives. Our daughters are aware of Juliet and hold her spirit in their hearts. I still have friends who remember each year and reach out to tell me they are thinking about me.

Additional Resource:
Share Atlanta—www.shareatlanta.org

Jennifer Davis lives in Marietta, Georgia with her family: husband (Lee), daughter (Maria, 7), and stepdaughters (Isabella, 17 and Francesca, 18). She works full-time in marketing and her husband works full-time as an attorney. They love to travel and do so as much as possible—both with and without the kids. Jennifer can be reached at jendavis626@gmail.com

I'll Hold You in Heaven
By Charisse Jimenez

It was a cold, rainy day in March. The pain was intense; it just would not stop. I walked, cried, prayed, and even crawled, but there was no relief. Little did I know I would endure this pain for a lifetime.

We had just moved into the house we had built. My husband and I had been married fifteen years, and we had three wonderful children. Life was good; things seemed to be falling into place beautifully. With the excitement of the move, I found out we were expecting! Nine years had passed since the birth of my last child. I placed little baby things, like a pacifier, booties, sleeper, and baby bottle in little pastel sacks. Each of the children, along with my husband, got a sack to open. The excitement that filled our home when they all realized we were having a baby was heartwarming.

Some time had passed and I wasn't feeling well. I went in for an ultrasound, and everything seemed fine. My baby was active, and the heartbeat was strong. But I felt like something was wrong. As I headed home, I saw a beautiful rainbow. I believed that was my sign from God that everything was going to be fine. That night I went into labor; the pains were coming so fast, and it was intense. I had never felt this kind of pain before. Nothing relieved it, so we headed to the hospital.

A few hours later, my water broke, and I delivered a stillborn baby daughter, Kiarra Alejandra. I was devastated. My children were devastated. This was something my husband could not fix.

We held her, kissed her, and tears flowed uncontrollably. She was so loved and wanted. How could this happen to me? I was numb. I was in pain. My heart ached when my milk came in because my body was trying to nourish a baby that was not with me. I had to leave the hospital with nothing but pain and empty arms.

I thought this kind of thing happens to other people. Well, to someone else, I was "other people." I did not leave the hospital with lots of baby things; I left with a baby-shaped hole in my heart. I went home and began her funeral. I picked out a pink coffin rather than beautiful baby bedding. We laid our baby Kiarra to rest at the footstool of her grandparents' resting place. We picked out a marker, not birth announcements that would proclaim we had a daughter.

Each day the reality became more and more real. I would dread the dark, and the morning sunlight. I struggled to put one foot in front of the other. I cried all the time and found myself clinging to the items I had purchased for my daughter's future. I wondered if I would ever be normal again.

My husband never knew what he would come home to. Would I be on the floor of my closet weeping? Would I be sleeping? Would I pull myself together for my family and fake existing? I hit different stages of grief at different levels. I often questioned—why did this happen to me?

I was a great mom. I loved my children and I had faith. I began to feel angry. I also realized I would never be the same. The hole in my heart would always be there. Nothing could fix that baby-shaped hole. Time would not heal that hole, contrary to the person who coined that phrase. Time does not heal all wounds. You never stop thinking about your child, and you long to hear your child's name.

Each year brings about a timeline that would have been your future. Five-year mark = kindergarten; eighteen-year mark = graduation. This year, my daughter would have turned twenty-one! I still wonder would she have been tall like her older sister? Would she have been feisty or funny like her older brothers? Would she have had curly hair like her younger brother? Would she have been mild mannered? Cheerleader or athlete? Those questions will always remain.

What I can say today is that I have grown from this journey. I have learned to maneuver my way around the baby-shaped hole in my heart. I empathize with others who are traveling this journey with me. I walk alongside many women who truly understand what this journey is like. I never knew that day twenty-one years ago that I lost my daughter, how many people would grace my life and would travel this journey with me. Some far ahead of me; some behind me; and some right beside me.

One year after my loss, I sat at a funeral of my older daughter's classmate. I knew what his mother's pain was like. Ten years later, I read the eulogy of my best friend's son, my godson. This past year, I prayed for a mother and her family as her baby battled cancer and lost his earthly fight. My heart was heavy for these moms, because I knew the journey they were on.

No words can make it better. No one can fix it. But I have learned, we can "show up." Showing up means making a meal, sending a card or text, saying a prayer, being a shoulder to cry on, going on a walk together and letting them cry, or getting angry, or even laughing. We must all grieve. There is no right or wrong way, and there is no time limit.

Today I am able to see the beauty of the journey I have traveled. I have been able to find hope and comfort that one day I will see my daughter again. I have learned that it is okay to laugh and even cry at any given moment. I still have a hole in my heart. I know deep sorrow—and unspeakable joy.

Losing a child is like no other loss. When we lose our parents, we lose our past. When we lose our spouse, we lose our present. But when we lose a child, we lose our future.

No matter what the situation surrounding loss, compassion and love are always needed. That compassion will be refined in you because of your loss. My baby's life was cut irreversibly short, but my love for her lives on forever. I know I will grieve for a lifetime. Losing a child is not one finite event; it is a forever, continuous, unfolding loss that spans over a lifetime.

Today, I am on the other side of grief—a horrible, agonizing, and painful grief, crushed along with all of my hopes and dreams for my daughter's future. Yet, still breathing, functioning, laughing, and finding beauty and gratefulness in each day.

I can tell you, it will come! Hope. Even the smallest flicker of hope will overwhelm you. Clinging to that ever so beautiful hope that you will be reunited with your child again one day can give you the strength to continue on. That hope will help carry you, even when your life seems to be reduced to dark ashes.

Learn to surround yourself with people who have stood in deep pain and searing loss, because they have willed their broken heart to beat again. Even with a hole in their heart, they have not bled out. They have found the tenacity to put one foot in front of the other, no matter how often they fell, or how painful the crippling walk was. They are our teachers, mentors, and guides, and they accompany us on this awful journey we have been thrust into. They are the friends you will realize, no matter how hard life gets, no matter how angry you feel, who will help carry you and never let you journey alone.

At this point in life, I have cared for so many who have battled their own illness and comforted the families of many who have lost loved ones. I suppose you could say I am seasoned, and I am thankful for what God has taught me along the way. Right now I have what I call a prayer door. My grandchildren come and we pray for the needs of others, and they contribute to the door. So many on the wall have battled illness, and some have lost their fight. One person on there lost his wife and baby in childbirth recently.

Here are a few resources that helped me
with my own journey:

I attended Rainbows for Children, a local support group for loss.

I searched for books that would help me understand my loss: *Roses in December,* by Marilyn Willett Heavilin. Many years later my favorite book, one I give away whenever I can, is *Waterbugs and Dragonflies* by Doris Stickney. This is the book I just recently gave to the mother of a two-year-old who lost his fight with cancer last month.

My favorite quote came after the loss of a dear friend of 40-plus years who lost her battle with breast cancer: " Stay focused on the beautiful and abundant things in life, even as illness carves more and more of what you love away." By Katrina Kenison

~Scripture~

God can bring peace to your past, purpose to your present, and hope to your future. John 14:27

I will not cause pain without allowing something new to be born, says the Lord. Isaiah 66:9

Trust in the Lord with all your heart and lean not on your own understanding. Proverbs 3:5

The Lord is close to the broken hearted. He rescues those whose spirit is crushed. Psalm 34:18

When you go through deep waters, I will be with you. Isaiah 43:2

Charisse Jimenez is the daughter of Dr. Donald Roy, RADM. She has traveled the world, military style. She married the love of her life, David Jimenez, thirty-seven years ago. She has an angel in heaven and raised four beautiful children, who have given them six adorable grandchildren. As a caregiver, she has held the hand of many as they took the hand of God. Sewing, cooking. and entertaining are her pleasures. Spoiling grandchildren is her gift! She can be reached via email: urasweetea@yahoo.com

The Grateful Eight
By Alicia Bertolero

When I add up the loss of children in my life, the number of eight losses and one who lived seems staggering. My abbreviated story: one stillbirth, one ruptured, ectopic pregnancy, five early miscarriages, and one ectopic pregnancy caught early. So, what made us continue to try for our miracle of birth?

We had been married for close to six years when I became pregnant with our first baby on July 3, 2011. Not many women know the exact date they conceive, but I have every reason to believe that July 3 was it. I just felt it, and I couldn't wait to take my first pregnancy test two weeks later.

We got our first positive test on July 18. I took my husband, Nic, to dinner and shared the news by presenting him with a tiny pair of shoes with flames on them. We were going to be parents!

The pregnancy seemed to progress in a relatively normal way; however, he was a little small for his gestational age so we got extra scans to monitor him. Never once did the doctor ever express serious concern; "He's just a little small so we want to monitor him." His anatomy looked fine.

He might have been just fine, but, unfortunately, I was sick.

I carried my son for just shy of thirty weeks. I went to bed one night with what I thought were Braxton Hicks and woke up the next morning knowing something was very wrong.

I felt heavy. When I got to work, I called my doctor's office and insisted I be seen that same day. I made sure that I buttoned up my responsibilities at work and left sticky notes everywhere "just in case."

I left work for my appointment. The NP performed the scan but would not allow me to look at the monitor. She clicked away, made digital notes, and then informed me that she had a difficult time finding the heartbeat, ". . . possibly because the baby was turned the wrong way." I knew this was a half-truth. You don't miss a heartbeat on an ultrasound at nearly thirty weeks gestation.

I was referred to another specialist since mine could not get me in right away. I picked up my husband from work and we went together. So many pregnant bellies in the room, all filled with life. . . smiling parents. As a new patient, I had to fill out several pages of paperwork. It felt like forever.

The specialist performed another scan, which also felt like an eternity. Why won't they just tell us the truth? Once the scan was complete, the technician turned to the other staff and instructed them to call "Angel Babies." I'd finally had enough and asked outright, "Is he gone?" I already knew he was gone that morning, but I needed to hear it. My amniotic fluid had disappeared, and it had happened within the last twenty-four hours with no explanation.

We were sent home. On the drive home, my doctor called from her home. Her voice was broken and compassionate. I was instructed to check into the hospital the next day. My womb was now a graveyard.

We checked-in the next afternoon as instructed and were put in the large room at the end where I would be induced. I learned later that there was a yellow rose placed on our door to alert staff of the situation. It broke my heart to know that there was even a protocol for this type of situation.

God had mercy on me; labor was relatively short. At 3:31 a.m., I gave birth to a sleeping little boy weighing 1 lb. 11oz. The sick irony is that exactly twenty-eight years before, my mom welcomed me into the world. My birthday gift this year was saying goodbye to my firstborn before I had even had a chance to say hello. This later turned out to be a blessing in my book; I have a special day that connects me with my son. We share the same birthday!

Two weeks later, the extensive labs came back from both doctors. I was diagnosed with celiac disease (an autoimmune disorder) and also found to have a serious blood clotting disorder. This little boy saved my life in his passing. It took me a long time to get over the guilt I felt that I survived and he did not.

The story doesn't end there

We tried again almost right away; we felt like we could handle it. I was five weeks pregnant, but I wasn't really. I was actually nine weeks along.

I went to bed with lower abdominal pain one night, figuring it was from early pregnancy ligament stretching or something like that. I was still feeling the dull pain the next day, but I went to work anyway.

It was Friday, June 22, 2012, and we had plans to drive up to Sacramento so I had the car that day (thank God!). I left work early to go pick up my husband around noon. On the freeway, I experienced what felt like a knife stabbing my lower right side. Every bump on the road was piercing. My fallopian tube had ruptured, and I was bleeding internally. I barely pulled up next to his work downtown; he literally carried me to the passenger's side and took me to Fresno Community's emergency room just down the street.

I lost over half my blood supply, my right fallopian tube, and almost lost my life. I thought I was fine with this loss emotionally because we had only known for about three weeks; I felt guilty that I felt nothing. . . until it unexpectedly hit me like a brick wall exactly one week later. I couldn't stop crying.

Then came our miracle

I told my husband in November that we were expecting number three. It was the third baby to share my uterus in one year. We had a good feeling about this one. We came home from the first official ultrasound and found a dove on the welcome mat in front of our door. We knew right away what to name him; he was our little "dove," Colm. Later on in the pregnancy, my husband and his dad were relaxing at their house when a mourning dove came and landed on my husband. I'm not really one to look for signs, but this was just unreal, like a kiss from God.

Our little dove, Colm Padraic Killian, was born healthy, at 7 lbs., 3 oz. on 7/3. (There's that date again!) Exactly two years after our journey started, on July 3, 2013, our miracle came full circle. We couldn't wait for the next miracle!

We are still waiting

We've had five more confirmed early miscarriages. I became quite numb after this and didn't bother asking God to reveal anything about them. I didn't want to accept this, and I felt deep shame that my body was so broken and couldn't do what it was made to do. Naming my babies would mean exposing my failures to the world and accepting that I was "broken," or so my logic went.

My health continued to decline. I was hospitalized for a week in February 2015 and diagnosed with Ulcerative Colitis (another autoimmune disease). I had the colon of a sixty-year-old.

Not long after, I recognized the patterns of another ectopic pregnancy, and sure enough, I had to have surgery for that one too. They were reluctantly able to save the tube, but I'm now considered very high risk for another ectopic. With my miscarriage history, there's also a high chance that I won't be able to carry anymore. Still, I wasn't ready to close the door just yet, so I insisted they not remove the only fallopian tube I had left if they could save it.

As weird as it sounds, I also consider infertility a loss. A mourning process has to take place before an infertile couple can adopt. I know that this is a reality we might be facing, but the door is still open.

The Redemption

Through these losses, I've made some tremendous friends. My friends know to reach out to me when someone they know experiences a loss, and I'll take care of them. These women and families have been some of the most amazing people I've ever met, and I would not have met them otherwise. Some are local, some are out of state, but we connect on such a deep level.

I've also gone through some amazing prayer ministry through my church and asked the Lord to reveal my children and their names to me. Here they are:

Padraic Nicolas: Reddish hair, handsome (we named him).

Penelope Maura ("Dream Weaver")—long, flowing, blonde pigtails, green eyes (I named her).

Ethan ("Solid, Strong, Enduring")—Tall, dark spiky hair, brown eyes.

Allison ("Noble")—blonde wispy hair, blue eyes. I envisioned her peeking over the fields of lavender in the heavens.

Adrian ("Water")—blond hair, blue eyes, similar to his sister Allison. I envisioned him with lots of energy and swinging from the trees.

Jonathan ("The Lord has given")—curly light brown or blond hair, freckles like his paternal grandmother, tall, and with a beautiful smile.

Avery ("To Confirm")—Curly black hair, and hazel green eyes like her dad, short like her mom.

Cormack ("Legend")—auburn hair, brown eyes, kind of short (hubby named him).

Naming my children and visualizing them as happy in heaven proved to provide much healing beyond that which I thought possible. I already knew they weren't sad or hurting, but visualizing them and naming them had a profound impact. I miss them terribly, and I'll always wonder who they would have become, but my perspective on these losses has made it easier to cope and experience joy again.

Alicia Bertolero lives in Fresno, CA with her husband and son. She does freelance ghostwriting for blogs and websites, and maintains a personal blog where she addresses issues surrounding pregnancy loss, health, autoimmune disease, and dietary challenges (www.suburbanhomesteader.com). She has hopes to pursue a career in personal training to help others who deal with similar health challenges. She can be reached at abertolero@sbcglobal.net

CHAPTER FOUR

LIVING WITH HOPE

A Happy Seed
By Danielle Lawhead

I've always envisioned what it would be like to be a mom. I had it planned out in my head so perfectly. When I found out I was pregnant, Justin and I prayed we would have a baby boy. Week twenty came so quickly, twenty weeks of a perfect pregnancy, and our dream of having a little dirt-filled faced boy turned into shopping for glitter and tutus.

February 11th was the moment we had waited for, the moment that every woman I knew prepped me for. Ten hours of anxiously waiting, and there she was. I had no idea what she looked like at first. Instead of that special moment you see on TV when the baby is instantly put on Mom's chest, all bloody and beautiful, and Mom is crying tears of joy with Dad kissing her on the forehead for a job well done, there was only a silence, followed with a faint cry. That faint cry was music to my ears, a sound that meant all was okay, followed by the doctor telling me they needed to take her to NICU to get checked out because her cry was faint and she looked a little pale.

Justin went down to the NICU to be with Taylor as they assessed her. I was in the room impatiently waiting to hold my daughter, cracking a smile with my dad as my sister and I were telling him all about the experience of giving birth.

When Justin returned to the room, that smile quickly turned into my heart dropping into my gut and tears pouring out of my eyes. I had asked Justin how Taylor was, and a man who is never lost for words dropped his head and shook it back and forth.

She was receiving an emergency blood transfusion, with monitors attached to what seemed like every inch of her chunky body, and a bubble C-PAP machine hooked into her tiny little nose. She had severe pulmonary hypertension and a hemoglobin of a four. After three weeks in the NICU, when we were finally able to go home, we thought we were leaving for good to start our lives together. But three weeks later, after concerned hemoglobin levels, we were right back in the NICU.

The doctors didn't understand why she wasn't able to make her own red blood cells. After a bone marrow biopsy, Taylor was formally diagnosed with an extremely rare form of mitochondrial disease called Pearson syndrome. At the time, there had been fewer than one hundred reported cases in the world. Like every parent, I immediately Googled it. There was not much to read, but there was one thing, "The life expectancy of a child diagnosed with Pearson syndrome is five years of age." Not my daughter, though. She was going to beat this.

I lived for the next two years in complete denial. Countless blood transfusions, tests, numerous overnight hospital stays, and specialists who had no idea how to treat her, and still I thought, *not her*. If you didn't know us, you would never guess Taylor was sick. You would never have known that this bright, beautiful, intelligent child was battling for her life every single second of the day.

Our precocious daughter would walk into the outpatient room for her transfusions with a smile and say, "thank you," after every poke and temperature check. God gave us a daughter who was mature and smart; for a two-year-old, her vocabulary was incredible.

She was certainly an old soul who could comprehend inflection and emotion. She knew when I was sad, unsure, and in doubt, placing my head in her lap while she would pat my head and tell me, "it's okay." Two and a half years of life, and there she was, dying right before our eyes.

After a month of being in and out of the hospital, the morning of June 2nd, felt like a typical day. Taylor hadn't been doing well for a few days; she was taking a turn for the worse. We were angry and scared. The doctor pulled us aside, asking us what we wanted him to do when her heart stopped.

We couldn't give up. Justin and I would leave together every day for an hour to shower and re-group while a family member would take a shift. In that time, I would cry; we would talk and hold hands, and Justin always told me it was going to be okay. I trusted those words every time he spoke them.

The nurse came in to check on her vitals. I looked up at her and said, "Is everything okay?" She replied, "I'm not sure."

I looked up and saw that Taylor's vitals had improved a little from the night before. I leaned over, held her hand, smiled, and said, "It's going to be okay."

That was it; she was gone. That fast. I didn't mean it was okay for her to go! I held her for four hours afterwards. I didn't know how to let her go.

Justin stood right by my side. Tears filled his eyes, but he was so strong. How was he so strong? The next few days the house was so silent, and then chaotic—overwhelmingly chaotic. Friends and family hovering over me to make sure I wasn't going to break.

I didn't know how I was going to hit a switch and change my daily routine of managing a full-time job and taking care of Taylor. She was my 24/7, my best friend; we were attached at the hip. But she was gone. Justin simply took my hand, kissed my forehead, and said the words that I knew were to be forever true, "I will not let you fall."

The day of Taylor's funeral, my sister had created this extraordinary video that captured every single moment of Taylor's life. If you didn't know her before, after that eleven-minute video, you did. You knew her smile, her personality, her spunk, her joy. She was pure joy.

While preparing the eulogy, one question she asked me was, "Why did Taylor love the Lorax movie so much?" The answer is simple: Taylor is *the seed*. She planted this happiness inside every single person she came into contact with. She brought our family closer together. She was a purpose!

Justin and I frequently remind one another of all the good she brought to our lives. Communication is such a huge part of overcoming this grief of missing her. The time when communication was lost, we were lost. Justin and I went through a few months of fighting and arguing. I felt like he didn't care. There were times when I felt like he wanted out now that she wasn't here to bring us together. I was so wrong. This man loves me more than words could ever describe.

There are so many times when Justin and I talk about what happened where I blame myself for not fighting harder. People always tell Justin and me that we are such extraordinary people for going through this tragedy, but they have no idea that even three years later, I grieve every day.

The truth is Taylor is the extraordinary one. She came into this life with no choice of what she was born with. She showed me what unconditional love really was so I could prove to myself that I was a good mom, the mom that I always dreamed of being. To prove that I can be depended on without running or throwing my hands up in the air; that I am strong.

This journey of grief is never-ending. In the end, how I choose to handle this is a choice—my choice, a choice that I will never take for granted. The two and a half short, most incredible years that I had with my daughter. . . a choice that I will no longer be afraid to just *be*. A choice to make a difference, to be someone's happy. A choice to no longer be afraid to walk in the gym alone because I will never take my mobility and health for granted again.

I will never take for granted the life that God has given me, the husband that he chose for me, and the two beautiful babies that he allowed me to enjoy. I've always known that Taylor was never mine to keep. She was simply an angel who was given a chance to change the world in a short amount of time. She planted a seed that will forever grow.

> **Danielle Lawhead** and husband, Justin, are currently in the process of setting up a nonprofit to help families with the financial responsibility of caring for a terminally ill child and to help fund research for a cure. Stay connected with us www. facebook.com/teamtot. Please feel free to contact them at DJFilbert@msn.com

The Sweetest Thing
By Dan Cope

I knew there was something special about Sean when I first saw him in the maternity ward. Then I thought, "No, you're just being a proud papa." As the years went by, I saw I was right. There was something special about this child. He was always smiling and always had something funny to say. All the kids in the neighborhood liked him and were constantly at the door, asking if he could come play.

His mother and I were beside ourselves with love and pride in our little boy. Then, at five, he was diagnosed with diabetes. He needed two injections of insulin a day to stay alive. I was nominated to administer the shots.

I took his little arm in my hand; I was trembling so badly. I had to stick a needle into him and couldn't bring myself to hurt him. I held his arm, and the needle hovered over it for what seemed like eternity. I just couldn't do it. Sean said, "Here, Daddy, I'll do it." He took that needle, stuck it in his arm, pushed the plunger and handed it back to me.

I couldn't believe this little five-year-old had so much courage. Every day he gave himself the injections and then went out to play or something. He was constantly besieged with insulin shock; we almost lost him a couple of times.

The nurse would stick that big IV needle in his little wrist and when she couldn't find the vein, she dug around until she finally found it. Sean's hand blew up like an inflated rubber glove and all he did was to calmly ask for help. I couldn't believe his threshold for pain. Inside, I was crying. Such a beautiful child didn't deserve this.

As he grew, I saw more signs of his special qualities. Everyone liked him. I was so proud. He never talked much about his diabetes, just calmly injected himself everyday. The diabetes was eating him up. His body was deteriorating before my eyes, and there was nothing I could do but stand there like an idiot and watch. I felt so helpless.

As time went on, his mother and I split up, and he wanted to live with me. I was with another woman who said she didn't want him around, so Sean and I walked out of her place onto the street with nothing.

My folks put us up until we found a room. He was having debilitating migraines at this point. He needed to be in a dark room so the light wouldn't affect him. This bothered my folks, who thought he should be in school or looking for a job. He didn't want to annoy them, so he would get on the subway and ride the train all day with his migraines, just to be out of their hair. That's how he was, always thinking of others.

One Christmas when I had no money or a job, I woke up to Sean having a reaction. I had no food and five dollars in my pocket. I went to the store and got him an egg sandwich. That was our Christmas. He never complained.

He went to California to be a counselor at a diabetic summer camp. He finished that and took his money to San Francisco where he and a friend were going to find an apartment together. His friend backed out, and Sean was on the street. He soon ran out of money and called me in New York City to ask if I could please send him some money.

I felt so bad for him, on the street with no money for food or medicine. I wired him three hundred dollars. My business as a cabinetmaker wasn't very profitable. I had to leave my apartment because the rents were skyrocketing. I was living in a little room in uptown. Sean called again, asking for some more money. I had just enough to get me a one-way ticket to San Francisco. I couldn't wait around to sell all my stuff, so I simply walked away from everything I owned and took a three-day bus ride to San Francisco to be with Sean.

I spent a couple of weeks on the street until my money was spent. I got into the carpenter's union and got enough to stabilize Sean and get us a room to live in. He was getting progressively worse, regurgitating streams of fluid while telling me, "I'll be okay, Dad. Don't worry."

That helpless feeling was killing me. In San Francisco he met a woman who was from Tennessee. She suggested they move to Tennessee where her family would give them a place to live, a car, and get them jobs. He went, and I missed him like crazy.

Eventually, they had a little girl. I was a grandpa! I was so excited when he asked me to come live with them in Tennessee so I could get to know my grandkids and be with him. An art collector offered to drive me there if I gave him my complete body of work, which I couldn't take anyway. I bartered with him.

In Tennessee, Sean had a job as a food preparer at a restaurant; I got a job washing dishes there. We had a shift together and I could watch him, with his weary, bright blue eyes, working hard to feed his family.

One day while I was doing dishes, the manager came and said, "You better go check your son." I went into the break room to see him in a chair and fluid all over the floor. He was about to pass out, so I called his wife to come help. I had to get back to washing dishes for fear of losing the only job I had while my son suffered. Once again, all I could do was watch helplessly. His wife came and got him and stabilized him with some glucose.

He was constantly in the hospital. He never let on how much suffering and pain he was in. He didn't want to bother anyone and felt he was a burden to his family. It was more added financial pressure with all his trips to the hospital and the expense.

I went to Massachusetts to visit my family. I had planned to pick up another car and get some extra money from my family to give to Sean to help him. While I was there, I got a phone call that Sean had died of complications from diabetes. He was only thirty-three. My feelings were mixed. I was grieving for my loss.

My brave little boy that I loved so much was gone. At the same time, I felt such relief that his pain and suffering was finally over. I remember his wit and charm, how he could go into any situation and lift everyone else's spirits even when he was the one who was sick.

I still talk to Sean every day. I don't know if he hears me, but I do it anyway. I had a dream a while ago. There he was, as a little boy. He saw me and gave me a big smile and we hugged. Just a dream? Maybe. . . maybe not.

I am now remarried. My new wife, Kathleen, has been a blessing in my life. This world is about suffering and learning how to cope with tragedies. I have been through many hard times and would have broken down a long time ago if I had not had the keys to salvation to help me along.

My own belief is that there is no death, only passing into another life. That gives me comfort, knowing I will see him again someday. I pray that when it's my turn to go, Sean will be there and we can pick up where we left off. Compared to eternity, this life is over in a flash; we need to learn our lessons while we have a chance. I find peace and strength in silence. Life is an adventure. The bad stuff only makes the good stuff sweeter.

> **Dan Cope** lives with his wife in Lincoln, Nebraska where he still works as a carpenter. He enjoys painting, traveling, and playing the guitar. Dan can be reached via email: dancope38@yahoo.com

Terminal Hope
By Juanita Arroyo

Our son, Anthony, was diagnosed with Fanconi anemia, a terminal illness, when he was two years old. It's a rare, genetic blood disorder that ultimately leads to bone marrow failure. Fanconi anemia patients are at high risk for certain cancers and other life-threatening illnesses.

I guess you could say that that is when I first mourned for Anthony. I knew he would have a lifetime of doctors, hospitals, and pain. I thought about all of the things I wanted him to experience in life, just like any mom. Would he live long enough to make friends, play sports, or fall in love? Would he have these important milestones? Sadly, most kids with this disease don't make it to adulthood.

He was healthy until he received a bone marrow transplant when he was six. How do you explain to a first-grader that life, as they know it, is basically over? After that, his health was more at risk as even a cold and fever could mean a hospital stay and continuous medications.

He had complications from his bone marrow transplant. Due to all of the medications he was on, including steroids, he developed osteoporosis and had to be in a wheelchair. The worst thing was seeing him suffer. He couldn't be the child he wanted to be. He couldn't do the things he wanted to do. The only thing he ever wanted was to be normal.

He was very open about his illness with people. Anthony educated his friends, nurses, and sometimes even doctors who were not aware of his condition. There were times we didn't know how to protect him. We couldn't put him in a bubble. We wanted him to live his life and experience things. He just wanted people to treat him like a normal child.

As a mom, my focus was always on taking care of Anthony first. For myself, I spent so much time praying. I had to be strong for him and tried to be positive. I had to keep my mind and body healthy for Anthony and my family.

Anthony was involved in the community. He was a spokesperson for the Central California blood center. He went to Washington, D.C. to speak to legislators so they would not cut funding on the bone marrow registry. He would stand up for other kids who were being bullied. He was positive and encouraging. I was so proud of how many friends he had and how many people he impacted.

At sixteen, Anthony was diagnosed with stage four squamous cell oral cancer. It was our worst nightmare. We didn't tell him it was stage four because he wanted to fight it, but radiation and chemo were not working. We wanted him to have hope that he could beat it, and we prayed for a miracle, even until the very end.

It was Anthony's decision to get treatment for cancer, and he chose to fight. He beat cancer and Fanconi anemia by the way he lived, the way he fought. He had cancer, but it never had him. Anthony fought a good fight and gave us all strength to fight alongside him. He gave it his all until his body could no longer wait for a miracle or a cure.

After being diagnosed with cancer, his friends from the school choir sent group texts and kept him positive and upbeat. At the hospital, he always had a roomful of people supporting him and cheering him on. We never left him alone. Someone was always there with him, especially at night.

Anthony's best friend, Kevin, would spend the night at the hospital with him. We told people that Kevin was our son so he could be at the doctor's office with Anthony. Anthony confided in Kevin that he was more worried about hurting us and leaving us.

Michaela Williams had been a friend of Anthony's since kindergarten. Due to his small size, Anthony was often bullied. Michaela always stuck up for him when others bullied him. When he was diagnosed with cancer, she came to see him at the hospital, doctor visits, or treatments. She was always there for him and often brought him gifts.

Anthony loved stuff animals. Michaela was going to give him a teddy bear on Valentine's Day, but he passed away the day before. We had him cremated and had the teddy bear cremated with him. It was Anthony's life that inspired her to create her own non-profit called "Cuddles for Cancer." They give blankets to children who are suffering from cancer. On the one-year anniversary of Anthony's death, Michaela and a group of volunteers gave 160 brightly-colored blankets to oncology patients at the same hospital where Anthony spent most of his life.

It wasn't just that we lost a son. Our family lost a nephew, a cousin; our daughter lost a brother. Kevin and Michaela lost a best friend, and his high school lost a valued classmate.

The most valuable lesson I learned from Anthony's battle was to never take life for granted. Always have faith, no matter what. Trust God. Our marriage is stronger now because we fought the good fight together. Our family is closer. Our daughter is even more precious to us now.

Through this process, I discovered my own strength. I didn't know what I could survive, even though I still struggle at times. No matter what you have to go through, you can still get through it and stand on your own two feet. You have no choice; your loved one is not returning. There are other people who need you. With Anthony's medical issues, I did anything to protect my family, including being strict on who came into our home with any type of illness, even one as simple as a cold.

A few things that helped me throughout the years, especially when he was diagnosed with cancer, were exercising, praying, reading books about Heaven, and watching the TV show *Proof*. Reading about near death experiences was comforting. I wrote in a journal about my day and my feelings—and also to Anthony.

Some of the things that continue to help me cope are simply thinking of him and recalling special memories. I love to watch his videos from his choir performances. It was a time when he was healthy, happy, and alive. I love hearing his voice and seeing how happy he was, in spite of his illness.

I had to make it to the one-year mark, which was extremely difficult. I felt if I could make it past the one-year anniversary of his death, then I knew I could make it through the second year, and the third. I had no choice. I realized the pain and void would always be there; I had to adjust and learn how to live with it.

We know someday we will see him again and find comfort that he is in a better place. We know that God healed him in His way, but we would have preferred to have him healed here with us on earth. Anthony, our hero, warrior, brave and courageous son, no longer suffers from pain, no longer needs medication, doesn't need a doctor, and doesn't have cancer or Fanconi anemia. Yet our lives will never be the same. We are living one day at a time.

We couldn't save Anthony, but we have kept his legacy alive. The Anthony Arroyo Memorial Scholarship at his high school has been established in his memory. In order to qualify, a student either has to be a member of the choir or Saint Baldrick's Club. The club raises funds by asking individuals to shave their heads to raise money for cancer research.

Anthony always loved doing fundraisers to help find a cure for Fanconi anemia. In October 2014, "Lighting the Path for a Cure" held its first fundraiser at Anthony's school. It was a very successful event. For every $10 collected, a light was lit that illuminated a strand of white lights, representing the path for a cure.

The most significant act that evening was when many people shaved their heads in honor of Anthony. He had lost his hair due to chemotherapy treatments. His dad, best friends, uncles and cousins—all shaved their heads. Anthony's wish was to continue to have fundraisers to help find a cure, and we continue to do so in his honor.

My best advice to any other parent who has a child with a life-threatening or terminal illness is to do what you need to do. Follow your gut and focus on what needs to be done to help your child. Deal with your emotions at your own pace, not based on what others think or tell you how you should feel. Process your emotions. Don't be in denial of the pain you are dealing with. You will never get over the pain; you just learn to live with it.

We looked for cures and better treatments for Anthony by contacting doctors on the east and west coast and in Germany. We kept in close communication with his doctors and educated ourselves on his disease so we knew the risks. We did everything possible. We prayed so hard for his healing and couldn't understand why his life had to be this way.

I often wondered how God could be so powerful to do such mighty things, but He could not heal Anthony. Then I realized that God did perform a miracle. He took Anthony home and healed him in Heaven.

Anthony Arroyo
Feb 13, 2015

Additional Resources:

For more info, please visit www.fanconianemiaresearch fund.com (FARF). They offer a camp for kids and education for parents.

For Michaela's charity, Cuddles For Cancer, please visit: www.CuddlesForCancer.net

Juanita Arroyo lives in California with her husband and daughter. For fundraising info or to donate to Anthony's scholarship fund, join the Facebook group: "Lighting the Path for a Cure".

A New Angel
By Megan Shank

My beautiful, blue-eyed boy was healthy for four years. He had eyelashes that would make a girl's heart melt.

That is until my son, Cash, started having migraines and vomiting. The motherly instinct quickly set in and off to the ER we went. We left the hospital with the assurance it was simply "a virus. Give him Tylenol; he'll be fine." That was not the answer I wanted, so I had a follow up appointment with a primary doctor. After a CT scan revealed hydrocephalus, we were told to drive straight to Children's Hospital.

Within the next few days, many tests were run. That's when we got the news that Cash had a rare brain cancer. It was unfathomable to learn, in the course of a few days, that there was a large tumor growing inside our little boy's head.

I was so angry at that stupid tumor. I wanted it to get out of my son! Now with our lives turned upside down, we were numb, but on a mission to find the best possible treatment for Cash. St. Jude Hospital was our choice. We couldn't have picked a better place.

With eight months of treatment, miles away from home, mentally and physically exhausted, I was willing to tackle whatever the next few months had in store. I would do anything to save my son.

It's a journey, watching your child fight for his life. The meds around the clock, the bags of chemo that had to be administered with the nurses wearing full body suits because it was so poisonous. And yet, that same dangerously poisonous bag was going into Cash's body to kill cancer.

Cash was often very sick and moody. Some days were horrible to witness as a mother. My heart broke every time as I helplessly watched the torturous treatments. I'm almost certain I suffer PTSD from witnessing my tiny son go through something so horrific. The flashbacks are still so vivid in my mind. We struggled. We were lost—broken and scared.

Through all of it, I learned how brave the little guy I gave birth to really was. He changed a whole community as well as people around the world. He stole everyone's hearts when he would look at people with his big blue eyes and say, "Do you want to do lunch, beautiful?"

Cash was one of the poster children for St. Jude Hospital. He asked that same question to Jennifer Aniston as they shot the Thanks and Giving campaign for public awareness.

He also did the chicken dance with Jimmy Fallon. They were both quite smitten with him. He fought hard. He loved. He lived, despite having to fight something so big. He was my hero. I could go on and on about how perfect he was in every way.

After a three-year battle with pineoblastoma, Cash lost his battle with cancer. Two years later, I still remember holding my six-year-old as he took his last breath. It happened on my thirtieth birthday. It feels surreal to celebrate your birthday, also knowing that's the same day your child went to be with God.

I try to look at it as a positive thing and that maybe that was his gift to me. Rob and I had both told him it was okay to close his eyes. We told him we would be okay. Now on this day, I will always know Cash went to Heaven, and he was my little boy again, cancer-free.

What is life like without him? There are no words. It's simply raw emotion. Some days I am still numb, even though it's been a few years. Life has gone on, but only because it has to. There are no outs in life, just some really low times. This can pertain to anyone, even though your battle may be different.

For a long time, I still looked in the rearview mirror to see if he was sitting in the back seat. I always do a head check before I leave the driveway. It is something I've always done since I had his older brother, Wyatt, when I first became a mom.

I thought I had this mom thing down pretty good until cancer. It wasn't as if I was dealing with my grief only; I also carried the kids' grief and Robert's grief. They were just as lost as I was. Then to juggle everyday life on top of that. . . Some days are better then others. Other days were barely tolerable. I'd like to say there have been more good days, but I'm honestly just not there yet.

I have heard it gets better in time, that you learn to coexist with the raw pain, but so far, time has just felt like another day added to the last time I've seen him. I do push myself to set the best example I can. I don't give up even when times are hard. I've always believed that is something that can really tell you about a person's character—how they handle themselves when life is really pushing against them. I feel like I have to be a good example because Cash is always watching.

He always wanted what was best for everyone. Even when he was as sick as he was, he made sure everyone was okay and we knew he loved us. I live life for him and for my family. He left behind a legacy, but it's my responsibility to continue to honor that legacy.

In honor of Cash, we do whatever we can to give back to St, Jude, including the dream home giveaways. This year will be the tenth year here in our hometown. Millions of dollars are made. And in the end, someone ends up winning a beautiful home for only $100 per ticket. I find it comforting to give back as much as I can after all they did for Cash.

Though still being human, I do have my days when I can't get out of bed. I take the time to cry, and I long to see his little face. It hurts my heart every day. There have been a lot of ugly days on this journey.

I see more and more kids dying because of cancer, including Cash's friends he met while in treatment. I ache knowing the pain these parents feel and what those kids also suffered. I keep myself involved and in touch with fundraisers for St. Jude, anything to help those sweet faces. They are so resilient.

They shine. Even on their weakest days, they smile. How can that not give me hope?

I find the greatest peace knowing he doesn't hurt anymore.

Megan Shank lives in Fresno, CA. She is the mom of three wonderful children. She hopes to keep her son's legacy alive. She continues to work with St. Jude to raise awareness and funding until a cure can be found. Megan can be reached via email at: m.shank1984@gmail.com. For more info on St. Jude Hospital, visit: www.stjude.org

The Smile That Warms Your Heart
By Celine Ford

In October 2003, we lost our precious daughter, Audrey, to viral myocarditis. Audrey was nine years old and a twin to Ashley. We also had a thirteen-year-old son, Nicholas.

Audrey's sudden and unexpected passing turned our world upside down. We had moved to California less than two years prior and had no relatives in the area. Though family and friends came from afar to help us in our grief, it is when everyone went back to their daily routines that I realized we would have to adapt and figure out what family would be like for us. During the first winter, I remember sitting on the couch at night; all four of us. It seemed no one wanted to be in a different room. Perhaps being close together was comforting.

Going back to work quickly was also important to me as I was a teacher in the school my children attended. My husband also returned to work within two weeks after Audrey's passing. We felt we needed to keep "normal" everything we possibly could. However, it became evident that we would never regain our "normal."

It was difficult to watch other families and just wish I could erase everything and be whole like them. But my family is what kept me going. We had lost a child but still had two who looked up to us for guidance. We spoke often, and still do, about Audrey.

To keep her memory and her name alive has been very important and soothing to all of us. We established a foundation at the Catholic school where Audrey was a fourth grader at the time of her passing. It is called "Let Your Light Shine" and provides tuition assistance to students who attend our school. This legacy has helped us feel like Audrey has made and will continue to make a difference in this world. It also keeps her story alive.

Though time has eased the pain, or perhaps we have become used to the pain, I still get caught off guard once in a while. It might be a song on the radio or something someone says, but suddenly I just can't hold back tears.

Probably the most painful time for me has been to watch Ashley miss her sister. The loneliness of a twinless twin has to be the most sorrowful emotion I have ever been exposed to. It is also something I can never comprehend, thus I have always felt helpless in supporting Ashley with that void. In time, we found activities, most of them ones that Ashley had not experienced with her sister. That way she could enjoy them without yearning for her sister. And in time, we have become accustomed to our new life.

There is laughter, happy moments, and celebrations in our house. We have learned that life is not promised for tomorrow. So we live each day as best we can. That is the best way we can honor Audrey's presence in our lives.

Celine Ford is currently living in Yountville, California with her husband Martin. She is teaching fifth grade and is vice-principal at St. John the Baptist Catholic School in Napa. She and her husband are the proud grandparents to Aubrey (born November 2015), daughter of their son Nicholas and Rosa, and her big brother, Angel. Celine can be reached at: celineford@ sbcglobal.net

*

Ashley felt like she should share her own experience and perhaps connect with others who have lost a twin. Here is what she writes:

I remember the last day with my twin sister as if it happened yesterday. We had only lived in California for a year and we were nine years old. We attended a Catholic elementary school and were in the fourth grade.

That week my sister had been fighting the stomach flu. On the morning of the day she passed, my mother would not let her go to our soccer game. She was really disappointed and wanted to go.

I remember she was taking a bath in my parents' room when I walked in and promised her we would win the game for her. She gave me a thumbs up and showed me one of her smiles that always warmed my heart.

I came home later that afternoon, excited about the fact that we had won. I practically ran into the house to tell my sister the exciting news. As I raised my voice calling for my sister, my mother told me to be quiet because she was sleeping. I remember looking at her on the couch as she slightly opened her eyes, looked at me, and then smiled.

That night, I was awakened by the voice of my mother yelling on the phone. My sister and I shared a room. I looked over to see that her bed was still made.

I lifted the covers off of me and walked out of my room, sleepy-eyed, to see what was going on. I saw my sister on the bathroom floor and my father giving her CPR. I was confused and did not understand what was happening.

I went back and sat on my bed trying to process everything that was occurring. Not much later the firefighters and then the EMTs arrived. One officer offered to drive us to the emergency room. We waited and waited in an isolated room the nurse had put us in until the doctor entered the room to tell us the news—something that would forever change our lives: my sister was gone.

From that night, I did not sleep in our room for months. Eventually, I moved back into our room. During that time, I developed a shiver at night. My body muscles would tense up and I would shiver constantly. I would be up at night for a good amount of time before I would get my mother to help stop it. This went on sporadically for several months.

We finally decided to go to the doctor, who told us I was having anxiety attacks. These only occurred in the evening when I would go to bed. After a few years, my panic attacks slowed down.

After moving back into my room, I started dreaming about Audrey. For a few years, I dreamt of my sister. There is one dream I remember the most: she was in our old house in Texas, wearing her favorite purple bathrobe. I approached her and said, "Didn't you die?"

To which she replied, "No, I am right here, aren't I?"

I continued, "But Mom said you went to Heaven."

She replied, "I am here with you and always will be."

After that, I smiled at her. She smiled back and I woke up. It was so real to me that I turned to my sister's old bed to tell her about the dream. Of course, I started crying when I realized that she was really gone. I think about this dream all the time. When I'm having a tough day, I think how she said, "I am here with you and always will be." It's something that helps me get by.

I started playing soccer again, but it did not last long. On my way to practice one day, I had a meltdown in the car. I told my mother I could no longer play as it was not the same without my sister. For a while I did not play any sports until a close friend from my class taught me basketball. From there I joined a basketball team. Playing a sport really helped me cope with stress and emotions. It also led to other things such as coaching, which I really enjoy.

After Audrey died, it was difficult for me; to this day, it still is. I was used to having someone there for me when I was having a tough day. She always would hold my hand when I was scared or sad and tell me it would be okay with that smile of hers. When I would have nightmares, she would let me crawl into her bed and sleep next to her. My sister slept like a rock; I always ended up hanging off the bed or on the floor, but it was still comforting to me.

She always helped me with my homework and cleaned our room. After she passed, I had to learn how to do everything myself. I had to learn how to do my own homework, clean my whole room, deal with my nightmares, and find a way to cope when being in a sad or scared mood.

All of it was hard; to this day I am still trying to learn how to cope with a rough day. I always picture my sister's smile, and somehow it makes things better. I think of the day when it will be my turn to go to Heaven; she will be the first to greet me with her smile. Her smile and who she was helps me every day.

It pushes me to be my own individual and embrace who I am, because my twin sister loved me for who I was. Even though I know I could have been a lot better to her, she still loved me and helped me when I did not deserve it. There is a line in the Kenny Chesney song "Who'd You Be Today" that says, "The only thing that gives me hope is knowing I'll see you again someday."

Audrey might not be with me here in person, but she is half of me and always will be. There will come a time and day that I will be reunited with her, but for now I will be my own individual and make my own difference in the world like she did.

Ashley Ford lives in the Napa Valley. She graduated in the spring of 2016 with a degree in viticulture. She was recently hired as an assistant winemaker and tasting room lead for a local family-owned winery. Ashley can be reached at: asford43@gmail.com

A Life's Journey
By Patrick Murphy

> "Having death constantly at our heels is what keeps
> us living."—*Claire Wineland*

Our journey with our daughter began the day we met
her in San Francisco with her adoption agent. Kayla was this
tiny, quiet, little four-year-old girl full of smiles and questions.
From the first day we met, it was a foregone conclusion that she
would become part of our family. She had been through seven
foster homes in one year prior to joining our family. That was
many transitions for such a young age. On November 22, 2000,
Kayla officially became our daughter. We celebrated our first
Thanksgiving and Christmas as a family.

Then in January, 2001, we received the news that Kayla
had cystic fibrosis and was being admitted to the hospital for
immediate evaluation. The adoption agency gave us a chance to
cancel the adoption. We immediately refused. We knew this little
girl had come into our lives for a reason.

That first night, as we slept in the hospital with her, I
promised her I wouldn't leave her, that I would be there with
her till the very end. Cystic fibrosis is a genetic pulmonary
disease brought about by both parents having a recessive gene
that doesn't allow the body to breakdown the mucous produced
naturally in your body. The prognosis is death. It means a
lifetime of increasing hospital visits, medications, and poor
quality of life.

So our story began with the knowledge of how the story
would end—with certain death. I guess you could say that is the
real moment that we mourned her loss. It felt so different from
the sudden news of the loss of a child. Either loss is horrific and
devastating to any parent, but it gave us an unexpected gift—the
chance to plan her life with purpose.

The biggest difference when dealing with a terminally ill child is that we knew the end was coming; we just never knew when. We understood that we were on borrowed time. We approached every day as if it were her last. We encouraged Kayla to live her life to the fullest. It was our philosophy that what happened yesterday was behind us, and Kayla needed to focus on today and the future. We can't change the past. I wish I could have changed the genetics that set Kayla on her course, but that was behind us at that point. We made a firm decision not to waste precious time worrying about the past. She took that time, instead, to focus on what she was going to do today and tomorrow to leave a mark on this world.

Kayla lived by that premise and lived as much of her short life as possible. As she got closer to the end of her life, she started www.mylifewithCF.com and a Facebook page under the pen name ElizabethM. She wrote blogs and talked with younger CFers to help them understand what they needed to know and expect from this terrible disease.

In her last year, she underwent a double lung transplant in hopes of securing a few more years of life as science progressed in finding medicines and possible cures. Through this all, she worked very hard to keep a positive attitude and continued the drive to live her life to the fullest.

As parents, it was our responsibility to pick her up and dust her off when circumstances seemed overwhelming and she wanted to give up. Life was not easy, but we made the most of the time we had together. In the end, doctors told Kayla and me that she only had a short time left; she was in both forms of rejection just five months after the transplant and that they could do nothing more for her.

She was at a hospital a few hours away from our hometown. She did her best to accept the grim news and decided that she wanted to return home to her own local Children's Hospital and die among her family, friends, and her dogs.

By that time, Kayla was eighteen, a legal adult, and those were her wishes. So they prepared her for transport home. Who would have known that, due to a mishap in transporting her home, she would be left without oxygen and slip into a coma in transport. She died twenty hours later, never being able to say goodbye to her mother or myself. Kayla passed away in our arms as we sat on her bed holding her with thirty of her family members and closest friends in the room. Our fourteen year journey came to a close with the ending of our story, just as we had somehow always expected it.

All I can share with anyone else who is trying to cope with the death of a child is that during this horrific time in your life, try to focus on all of the positive times you and your child had during their brief time on this earth. Don't get caught up in, "I should have done this," or "what if I did this?" If you are a religious person, don't get stuck on blaming God, or asking "Why did you do this to me?" Rather focus on why God gave you this gift in your life, because when it comes down to it, a child is truly a beautiful little gift to you as a parent.

We chose to celebrate Kayla's life at her funeral. We then let her friends run the mass and had a celebration of life to share stories and laugh and cry about all the good times we had with her being part of our lives.

I would encourage anyone who reads this book to consider focusing on all those great times you and your child spent together. Focus on their life and not on the finality of death. When we have a sick child, we often focus so much energy on fighting their sickness that we forget that they are kids and need to have fun and enjoy life.

Don't let their death outweigh their life and all the special memories and gifts that you received. Your child would want you to go on with your life and continue to live it. That doesn't mean that you will ever forget them, but that they are helping you heal and live life as you have taught them.

I'd like to share an example of what I mean by this. I had a gentleman say to me after Kayla's death, "What a relief it must be to have the burden of a terminally ill child off your shoulders." It took all the strength I could muster not to punch the guy. He didn't understand that Kayla was a gift, and she brought joy and happiness into my life.

All the visits to the hospital, the medications, and the treatment were nothing compared to her laugh, her smile, and the love she shared with everyone.

I sometimes wondered what Kayla's life would have been like had she not found our family. Would she have had the same quality of life? Would she have been encouraged to live her life every moment of every day?

Looking back, I can see the perfect path of her life's journey, and I am so grateful that she ended up in our lives. I truly thought we were the ones who were helping Kayla the day we adopted her. However, now I know that she was the one helping all of us.

Her life continues to impact others. We continue to focus on her life, her spirit, and the lessons that she taught all of us.

Additional Resources:

Kayla's original blog: www.mylifewithCF.com

Scholarship @ University of Santa Clara: Kayla Murphy, Fine Arts Department

Facebook: Elizabeth M Cfr

Donations: Valley Children's Hospital, Madera, CA: Kayla Murphy endowment fund

Patrick Murphy lives in Fresno, California and is an Ag consultant. He dedicated his life to being a loving father to Kayla, his only child. He can be reached at: murphy.patrick.michael@gmail.com

SUDDEN SHOCK

Tolerating Shrapnel
By Janet Burroway

Every suicide is a suicide bomber. The intention may be absolutely other—a yearning for peace, the need to escape, even a desire to spare the family. Nevertheless, the shrapnel flies.

My husband, Peter, and I had been to a movie. We'd barely stowed our things when the phone rang. Our daughter-in-law, Birgitt, halfway round the world in Africa, said, "Didn't you get my messages?"

I fumbled, apologizing, "Oh, I hadn't checked."

Her voice blank, Birgitt said, "Tim has shot himself."

I replied, "How badly is he hurt?" I saw him hunting on a game reserve near their home in Namibia. My first image was of a bullet hole in his foot. I remember that in this image the foot was, absurdly, wearing a sock. I called to Peter, "Get on the phone! Tim has shot himself!"

He picked up the receiver and said, "How badly is he hurt?"

It was not many seconds before both of us took in the mortal contraction, "He's gone," and not many seconds after that when we understood that this going had been his intention. In some acid reflux of emotion I said to myself: *I knew it; more than once he said he would die young; I won't mind much.*

137

The end of the story is the most important part. We can't help it. It happens willy-nilly—the last sentence echoes backward through all the rest. You cast back over the scenes to understand how the parts fit together, how character and chance and history converged, what clues you missed, how differently this or that scene looks in the light of what happened after. It isn't a question of drama or surprise, I said, but resonance and rightness. Now I see that, working backward from the end of Tim's story, trying to understand it, I run the danger of reading suicide into every incident, distorting the meaning of his life toward its heartrending close. I accept that part of the job of grieving is to search, research, try to reach some minimally satisfying sense of why it must end this way. What is hard is that all the old stories have changed their point as well. Every one of my mother-memories is skewed and spoiled.

A small instance: I sat on a step in the breakfast room in my robe, an abounding ashtray beside me, waiting up for seventeen-year-old Tim, to whom I had recently given his first car. He appeared at 4 a.m., shoes in hand. I flipped the switch and scared the daylights out of him; I might as well have brandished a rolling pin like a shrew in a cartoon. Next day I spoke of it to a friend who put an end to such scenes by saying (always the punch line of this anecdote), "Not many of them kill themselves. And no mother ever prevented it by waiting up."

After we hung up, Peter and I huddled together. I said, "This is the big stuff." I don't know whether it struck me then that this was Army talk, throwaway; the thing Tim would have said.

"Yes, it is." He held me. We didn't sleep. We spent the next hours in that strange after-state of catastrophe, at once numb and intense, the body somehow silently thundering.

It was five o'clock when I called Tim's brother, Alex, to repeat the news. Unlike me he wept immediately, fully, blubberingly; and I sat in my vibrating space envying him that.

Tim was one of those boys for whom the paraphernalia of war held a fascination from toddlerhood. Guns, tanks, camouflage, planes—he learned commitment with model glue on the tip of a toothpick, and, unlike most boys, he never repudiated his first ambition. He spent three years in ROTC, four in the Army, and eight in the Reserve during which he volunteered for every available deployment. During this last assignment, he coordinated a project in mine removal from the embassy in Windhoek, clearing the detritus of the Namibian—Angolan war as a humanitarian gift of the United States. It was there that Tim met Birgitt. When his deployment ended, the Army decided no longer to staff his position, which would belong instead to the company that handled the field operation. So Tim came home to Florida and spent six months waiting for clearance to return to the same job as a civilian.

I was not afraid for him. I was adamantly against the war, but Tim and I had been on opposite political sides for most of his thirty-nine years, and we had learned to walk that minefield very well. Tim was committed to military values, and we were committed to each other. When he told me he was heading for Iraq, I said, "You know how lucky I feel, don't you? That you're taking mines out of the ground instead of putting them in? I know you'd put them in if that's what you were asked to do; I just think I lucked out you're doing this humanitarian thing."

He laughed. "I know, Mom."

There was no sign of depression. He said he was going back to Iraq for another six weeks only. He would be home in time for his fortieth birthday. It was too hard to be away from Birgitt and Thyra—and even his stepson, Neal, who was becoming "a typical teenager, foul-mouthed and recalcitrant"—within, we divined, a more or less normal range. Peter and Tim bantered about whether boys or girls were more exasperating in the teen years.

In six weeks he would be home safe. How many times did he tell me—warn me—that he was ready to die for his country, rushing full tilt and willing into battle? How can it have come about that he died violently at home?

Engorged with these speculations, I remind myself that Tim was drawn to the cheap and fragile toys of World War II before he could read, before we owned a television, before he suffered a concussion or endured his parents' divorce. Nor is there any doubt that the military offered him an adrenaline rush that could not be matched by the living room. Drawn to test himself to his limits, he was equally drawn to the rules that would place that daring in a noble system. Though it may seem that the yearnings toward risk and rules are at odds, and the ideas of hierarchy and community likewise, nevertheless that is what he sought and what the Army offered: extreme sport within an apostolic structure.

Tim had once told me, ". . . the warrior spirit . . . isn't directed at self and it isn't devoted to money. It needs an extreme integrity." He believed thoroughly in Honor, Duty, Country. . . The family has yet to understand this final act.

"*The trouble with dying,*" my brother writes, "*is that everything dies. We lose not one loved one but all of them at once. We lose the kitchen table with the newspaper spread on it. We lose the half-empty jar in the fridge and the memory of the jam we have eaten and the anticipation of the jam that is left. We lose . . . the sight of birds sliding on the wind. We lose the yellow line down the center of the road . . .* "

To have suffered so near a death as that of a child puts you in intimate connection both with the precious past and with your very long future as *nothing.* Old songs and brutal news make you bump up against the prospect of fatality; the face in the mirror unflatteringly speaks of the sloughing of this mortal coil, but though religion labors to deny it, the passage *into,* for yourself or your lost loved one, is fundamentally denied.

What does it mean, "to heal"? What does it mean, "You don't get over it, you get used to it?"

A friend, in the first six months of forever after the death of her partner, is offended by the idea of healing. *It's a wound,* she says. *It doesn't heal; it can still open.*

We tend in America to look for change in epiphanic moments. We want the instant diet, the meteoric success, the Ravishing, an Aha! of healing. But *moving on* is not a sprint, and not really a triumph of the human spirit. It is the doggedness of the world at your doorstep, doggedly knocking. One day you find you have read two consecutive paragraphs. One day you find you are angry not at the universe but at the local bank. One day you laugh, and quickly apologize to the beloved dead. One day a memory comes back shorn of grief, bearing only sweetness.

One solider carried several shards of shrapnel in his legs and torso. He said he could go for long periods unaware of them. But bending a certain way he would feel the jab of alien metal. In extreme cold the edges sung. The loss of Tim is like that, still sharp although the scar has closed around it. Most of the time I move forward comfortably in an ordinary life. But sooner or later in the course of an ordinary day, I will happen upon a place, a person, a memento—and the shrapnel bites.

I offer my friend the image of embodied shrapnel, which she accepts, guardedly. It doesn't feel like the truth to her. At six months, the wound still opens.

Halloween evening I was sitting at the computer at the kitchen desk. Peter's former wife, Jeanne, called to say that Anne (Peter's daughter) had been in an accident. She was hospitalized in Georgia, but being flown back to Tallahassee Memorial. A "life flight," Peter told me, a term I'd heard only on TV. I did not immediately register its inverted meaning.

In any case, we waited. Then the phone tolled.

He said: "No-o-o-o-o! What do you mean we've *lost* her!? Do you mean she's dead!?"

He hunched over the counter in a smart new swivel chair. I went awkwardly to him and awkwardly bent my body over his, like a hulking house, not comfort enough. He sobbed.

I remembered how Alex had immediately cried at hearing of Tim's death, and again I envied that capacity.

We flew back to Tallahassee to lay her to rest (*What? In the ground!?*) and went through the formalities of death again. We added her name to the plaque on the park bench at Lake Ella that we had dedicated to Tim. Anne may have run a stop sign; she was hit in the driver's side by a van, whose six occupants were drinking but were not much hurt. Her air bags did not deploy.

Now it was my turn to be the rock. I had to learn that not everyone spills sadness in words, and that for Peter silence was soothing, distraction best. He took solace in routine, and food, and family. *Why have we lost two of our three children*? Because one lived with guns and the other, in Derek's words, "had a heavy foot and was easily distracted." Because we could take it. Because everybody has a short story or a long. Because death is certain and also arbitrary.

The statistics of survival for the marriage of a lost child are grim. We were "lucky," if that can be said, in that each of our children belonged to a former marriage, and so there was no impulse to blame each other for the loss of either. We were "lucky" in that the deaths occurred in tandem, so that each of us was able to be strong for the other. We were lucky—no quotes— in that we had each other.

My surviving son, Alex, and wife, Tricia, are ensconced with the girls in their new South London house, where we continue to visit them every year. He tells me that his sense of loss increases rather than diminishes, that as the years pass he misses not only his brother but being a brother, living as what he never was or was meant to be, an "only child." Nevertheless, he writes, "I do feel that I've come to a peace with it. I do talk to him sometimes. Just the odd comment when I wish I could have shared something with him. There's little comfort in these vaguely melodramatic moments, but the repetition and rhythm of life draws you away from pain, and in its absence you heal. I think this is one of the reasons why humans are so drawn to music. It's a prehistoric attempt to imitate life and nature, and so to seek solace in that synergy."

A few years ago there was a vigil in Tallahassee. Little Lake Ella was to be surrounded by candles, one each for the dead soldiers of Iraq and Afghanistan. On the afternoon they were preparing, I went to the organizer, explained my mission, and asked if she could add a candle for my son. Of course. She wrote *Tim* in black felt tip on a paper bag, filled it with sand and wedged a little taper in the sand. At dusk I helped to light the candles. The lake covers perhaps six acres. The flames surrounded the whole of it, with inches between the bags. There were no speeches, no demonstrations, no taking of sides, just neighbors walking around the lake at dusk in shorts and sandals, with dogs, push chairs, children climbing the live oak for a better view. Later I must ask myself why, when I never wanted Tim to be part of the Army when he was alive, I was so comforted by his being included among the dead: the paper bag, the sand, the candle in the ring of light.

Grief is not the same as depression, can be in stunning ways its opposite. Depression leeches everything of joy, of purpose, of interest. I remember, depressed after my first marriage ended, thinking that the effort of putting my shoes on was more than I could bear. I shook through the aisles of grocery stores unable to buy milk, bread, meat. I lay on the floor unable to feel anything but the twisting of my stomach. I thought that everyone who seemed happy was merely duped. I was *unselved*. But for me, grief does not operate that way. It can be intense. Ugly, awful, wracking. Intense. The things I've always enjoyed I still enjoy. The world still offers its extravagant haberdashery of beauty, boredom, love, and weather.

Walking one afternoon, I came to understand that *loss* is another word for *longing*. At some point you realize that more of your life is behind you than ahead. You were told to "live in the moment," but you almost never did. On the contrary, the moments were tainted by wishing they would pass, or regretting the past, or anticipating something more wonderful. It's now, in retrospect, that their luminous significance is revealed.

There is no stilling of the inevitable *what if*. If Anne had crossed that intersection thirty seconds earlier; if I had called Tim that Friday afternoon . . . but it is also possible, now, to feel that his life and hers are finished stories. Tim is no farther from me than he was in Africa, and in some ways nearer. I can imagine him as an adult in rooms he inhabited as a child, and in rooms now familiar to me that he never saw. I make him. I make him up.

And when I look up from my desk I still see among the pictures of those I love a grainy black and white image of an Iraqi father prostrate over the coffin of his son, with whom I have more in common than with the heroes of my own country, just as I have more in common with the mother of a Hamas suicide bomber who, dismayed at her grown son's political choices, is caught with no option but to let him go wrong-headed to his death.

And all over the world is a slender web in space and time, of people whose lives were changed, or who were born at all, because my son who loved weapons went, by the hazard of history, into the odd profession of getting rid of them.

And in that sense, there is no end to his story.

Janet Burroway is the author of plays, poetry, children's books, and eight novels including Pulitzer nominated *The Buzzards; Raw Silk, Opening Nights, Cutting Stone* (all Notable Books of *The New York Times Book Review*), and the 2009 *Bridge of Sand*. Recent works include the plays *Division of Property, Sweepstakes* and *Medea With Child*, which have received readings and productions in Chicago, New York, London, San Francisco, Hollywood, and various regional theatres. *Parts of Speech* was the 2014 winner of the Brink award from Renaissance Theatreworks in Milwaukee. Her most recent play is *Boomerang,* a modern take on *Lear* for the Sideshow Theatre Company in Chicago. Her *Writing Fiction,* now in its ninth edition, is the most widely used creative writing text in America, and *Imaginative Writing* is in its fourth edition. Her children's book *The Giant Jam Sandwich* has been translated into twenty languages and scored for orchestra. She is author of a collection of essays, *Embalming Mom* (Iowa, 2009) and the memoir *Losing Tim* (Think Piece Press, 2014), and editor of the essay collection *A Story Larger Than My Own: Women Writers Look Back at Their Lives and Careers* (U. Chicago, 2014). Winner of the 2014 Lifetime Achievement Award in Writing from the Florida Humanities Council, she is Robert O. Lawton Distinguished Professor Emerita at Florida State University.

Losing Tim can be ordered as an e-book or paperback from all major bookstores and online via: www.thinkpiecepublishing. com or www.janetburroway.com

My Only Child
By Steve Roberts

"Spirited." If I could use one word to describe my only child, this is the word I would choose. Kelsey Marie Roberts was born November 22, 1993. I will never forget seeing her for the first time in the delivery room. I exclaimed, "Look at all of that hair!" as she was entering this world. Kelsey was born with dark brown hair and brown eyes. She was my pride and joy. I loved her with all my heart. I spent as much time with Kelsey as I could so that I could be the best father possible. I loved to carry her on my shoulders until she became too heavy to lift over my head. As Kelsey grew older, I discovered she was also a great photographer. She took some amazing pictures when she and I went on vacation the week before she was murdered. I use some of the pictures as wallpapers on my computer.

Four months before Kelsey was killed, she met the reigning Miss Texas and received an autographed picture from her. Miss Texas wrote, "Kelsey, never give up on your dreams." Sadly, the opportunity for Kelsey to pursue her dreams was violently taken from her on Friday, August 5, 2005.

It is a day that I will never forget. My ex-wife and I were going through a divorce and had shared custody of Kelsey. When I arrived at my ex-wife's house to pick up Kelsey, I called her cell phone and rang the doorbell, but she did not answer. I decided to call one of my ex-wife's friends who happened to have a key to the house. The friend went inside while I waited outside; soon after, the friend came outside and told me to call 911.

I later learned that my ex-wife had smothered Kelsey with a bed sheet. The toxicology report also detected traces of Ambien in Kelsey's bloodstream. My ex-wife had used a kitchen knife to carve a five-sentence suicide note into the top of her dining room table. She also took a large quantity of sleeping pills and slit one of her wrists. When the police arrived, they found my ex-wife in her bed asleep. The sheets were covered in blood. She was taken to a local hospital and remained in an unconscious state for almost a week. When she regained consciousness, she was transported to the county jail.

She was put on trial for murder in July 2006 and was found guilty. She is currently serving an eighty-year prison sentence and will be eligible for parole in 2035, when she will be seventy-nine years old (if she lives that long). My ex-wife has never spoken publicly about what she did, nor did she speak during or after her trial.

As you can imagine, I had many unanswered questions. I hate the word "closure." There is no real closure, no resolution, when you lose a child, especially to murder. It can be an unrealistic expectation that we have as parents when we lose a child.

It's been eleven years since I lost Kelsey. I've had many years to process the shock and have found there are a few things that have helped, as well as some things that have made it worse. I have come up with five "F's" that have been pivotal in coping with her loss.

Faith

If I didn't have my faith, I think everything else would just crater on me. My faith gives me hope that I will see Kelsey again, and it will be for eternity.

Family

My family has been very supportive. My sisters send me cards on Father's Day. That is one of the toughest days of the year for me, especially because Kelsey was my only child. For years following Kelsey's death, I questioned my purpose since the responsibilities of being a father had been taken from me. But I am, and always will be, Kelsey's father.

Sometimes, I can't explain what I'm feeling when I have a bad day. It helps to talk with others who have gone through it. When people think of me on Father's Day, her birthday, and the anniversary of her death, it helps me feel supported. It's important for friends and family to know this as they often think a bereaved parent doesn't want to talk about it or that by talking about their child(-ren), it will bring us down. I love talking about Kelsey and remembering her.

At a family gathering soon after Kelsey was killed, one of my family members tried to encourage me to have fun and join a group on the dance floor, but all I could think of was going to the Daddy/Daughter dance with Kelsey. At one time, the event triggered good memories, but they were now painful ones. I wasn't ready to dance, and the family member needed to understand that. And that is okay. I can talk about Kelsey and remember her and not get emotional or break down. That's the most important thing for others to understand if they know anyone who has lost a child. Talk with them about their child; don't ignore their child or be afraid to bring him or her up, especially on anniversaries and holidays.

Friends

I have connected with many other people who have experienced similar challenges. One man lost his daughter four years ago, and our daughters' death anniversaries are one day apart. I reached out to him at a support group meeting, and we now attend concerts and sporting events together. I value his friendship and would not have connected with him if it weren't for Kelsey. I'm amazed at how she is still connecting me to people all these years later.

Future

It always helps to move forward in life, when you have something to look forward to. One day, I was watching a minister on TV and he spoke about the analogy of perspective. He equated it to looking through the windshield in the front of the car (to looking forward) and a small mirror to look behind us (to scan the past). The message was that the future view has a much bigger space to see out of. We should keep our past small in hindsight. The key is to focus on the "bigger picture" of what is ahead of us and not on the past.

Forgiveness

Nelson Mandela said, "Resentment is like drinking poison and then hoping it will kill your enemies." I use that quote often, especially when I speak at grief conferences and chapter meetings.

I have chosen to forgive my ex-wife for murdering our only child, but I can never forget. I chose to forgive as a gift to myself, but I have never spoken to her about it directly. Since I am not the murder victim, could I forgive someone for doing something to someone else?

I remember when reciting the Lord's Prayer, I would say the line "Forgive us our trespasses as we forgive those who trespass against us." I couldn't exactly add a footnote that said, "except my ex-wife." It felt hypocritical to say the prayer and forgive everyone but her.

Healing With Hope

One of the things that I do to honor Kelsey is to provide college scholarships to graduating seniors at the high school Kelsey was to have attended. I also provide financial assistance for other families at the private grade school that she attended for four years.

One of the activities I became involved in after Kelsey's death was participating in 5K events. I had never run long distances, so I got myself out of my comfort zone and attempted to complete a 5K. I succeeded in achieving my goal and realized that there is still fun to be had without feeling guilty.

Additional Resources:

Alive Alone is a nonprofit organization for bereaved parents who have lost their only child. www.alivealone.org

The Compassionate Friends is a national nonprofit organization for parents and grandparents who lost a child and for surviving siblings. www.CompassionateFriends.org

The National Organization of Parents of Murdered Children is an organization for the families and friends of those who have died by violence. www.pomc.com

Steve Roberts lives in Texas. He has connected with many other bereaved parents and speaks at local support group meetings and national grief conferences around the country. He values the many people he has met in Facebook groups and connecting with people. He started a 501(c) 3 organization to provide financial assistance and college scholarships in honor of Kelsey. Contributions can be made to The Kelsey Roberts Scholarship Fund at any Bank of America location. Steve can be reached via email: sjroberts1216@hotmail.com

The Power of Choices
By Debbi Rath

I am a trained paramedic and have worked in emergency response since 1993. My job is to respond to 911 medical and trauma calls. I am also a mom who had two children, Merissa and Garrett. My son, Garrett, was 6'3" and 240 pounds. He was a gentle giant who played soccer, baseball, and basketball. Friday and Saturday nights, you would usually find him four-wheeling in the mud or hanging out with friends. He would truly light up the room with his presence. He always made friends easily. He and his girlfriend of three years, Melissa, were inseparable.

Garrett loved country music and making people laugh. He did great impressions of Jim Carey, Jeff Foxworthy, and many others. He loved big trucks with big tires and working on them was his passion. He would chase ambulances or fire trucks just to ask, "Do you know my Mom?" He was so proud of me and the job I did. He was my biggest fan.

On February 26, 2004, I received a phone call that no mother or parent ever wants to receive. I was told that there had been an accident on the freeway. The person on the other end of the phone said, "You need to get here". My heart dropped and I felt the color drain out of my face. I thought I was going to throw up. That was the beginning of my worst nightmare. I knew it was bad. Where was Garrett? Why hadn't he called me? All I can remember is that it felt like a bad dream. I kept hearing someone screaming. And then I realized it was my own voice I was hearing. My body felt like it had been turned inside out.

As we approached the scene of the accident, it was a scene all too familiar to me because of my job. I saw death every day. But I was not the paramedic on call that day. It wasn't someone else's family member or child. It was mine. All the red lights flashing against the night. . .all the traffic, people everywhere running around, chaos. Then I saw it. . .the yellow CHP blanket lying on the road. I instantly knew that was my child lying under that blanket on the cold asphalt. I jumped out of the car and ran as fast as I could until a CHP officer caught me. All I wanted to do was hold my son. I just wanted to make things better for him. I wanted to tell him that I love him and that everything would be all right, that Mom was here.

Then I saw a man with another CHP officer being put through a sobriety test. He was failing the test. I saw the handcuffs go on that man and then he was gone. My shock turned to anger. That man just killed my son. How is it that he can walk away and my son can't?

Garrett was a passenger in his best friend's jeep that had just gotten out of the repair shop four hours prior to the accident. The jeep malfunctioned and spun out of control on the freeway, coming to rest facing the wrong way in the slow lane. Luckily, they didn't collide with anyone else. A tow truck was right behind them and stopped, putting on overhead emergency lights to warn any other vehicles that there was a hazard ahead. Due to one driver's impaired vision from the alcohol he consumed, he failed to slow down and blew by the tow truck going 75 m.p.h. He swerved and struck Garrett in the back, throwing him approximately 114 feet down the freeway with a force so hard that one of Garrett's shoes landed in the northbound lane. In the police report, the driver stated that he heard and felt two "pops." He thought it was his tire popping. He then lost control, never hitting his brakes, and his vehicle rolled over down the freeway. Yet the driver was completely unharmed. One of those pop sounds was him hitting my son.

The autopsy report stated that Garrett was dead from multiple blunt trauma before he even hit the asphalt. I stood on the roadside for nearly 2 ½ hours crying as my son lay on the cold, wet asphalt under that glaring yellow blanket.

I would not leave until they let me see my son. They told me it was a crime scene, and I could not see him or touch him. I was finally allowed to see him. I just needed to see if his eyes were open or closed. I needed to see if he was at peace. I prayed that he felt no pain, that there was no time for fear in his last moments. I just desperately wanted to hold my son and tell him it would all be okay.

I don't remember the ride home that night. But I remember walking in to Garrett's bedroom and crawling into his bed, hugging all of the pillows. I wanted to wake up from this horrible dream. I never wanted to get up again. But I had to. I had to make funeral arrangements, write an obituary, pick out a casket, pick out a cemetery plot, pick out the last outfit Garrett would ever wear, pick out a headstone, making sure the inscription was perfect.

Having to say goodbye and kissing Garrett for the very last time while he lay inside a casket is something that I cannot even put into words. I slept in Garrett's bed for three weeks and then I locked the door. I could still smell him, his cologne, his clothes, see the last things he wore and the last things he touched. It was all so tangible. I didn't want that to ever go away.

I light a candle for Garrett every day. I write to him in my journal and ask him to help us through this nightmare and to give us some of the strength that he had so much of. I tell him how much I miss him, how much I love him, and how proud I am that he is my son and I am his mother. Garrett was not only my son, but he was my buddy, my pal, and my friend. He was a social butterfly and a friend to everyone. He was someone you could always count on, day or night.

Garrett was only nineteen years old when he died, yet 600 people came to his funeral. That is how many people he had already touched in his short lifetime. I can only imagine how many more lives he would have enriched had he been alive today. Alcohol and a drunk driver took Garrett's life away from him. That one pop took Garrett's hopes and dreams away from him in an instant. We will never see him marry. We will never get to hold his children.

Garrett and I had a relationship so few ever get to experience. We were very close. He checked on me every morning and would call me throughout the day just to say hi and tell me that he loved me. He would leave funny messages on my phone, always making me laugh, and always ending each call or text with "I love you, Mom." He would come in my room and sit on my bed and tell me about his night before or how his day went. He would go to the grocery store with me and just spend time with me. He would tell me never to worry about life, that he would always take care of me, that he would always be with me.

I know that many parents don't have that type of relationship with their teenagers. I was truly blessed and grateful to have that. But on that day, my life changed forever. Now, all I have is memories. I have no future with my son.

I will never be the same person I was before. I had to take a leave of absence. My marriage ended. Depression and loneliness became my two best friends. I had to take medication to be able to sleep at night. I can't begin to explain the pain that I lived with every day, every moment, every second. There are no words to describe the devastation, the heartache, and the pain that can drop you to your knees at any given moment. There were times it hurt just to breathe. There were many times that I didn't even have the strength to simply take another breath.

Eventually, I went back to work full-time. Going on trauma calls was harder than ever. I could personally relate to the parents and families who were left behind. There were some days that it took everything I had to get out of bed and face the world. There are other days I was so angry and tried so hard to hold it together, like a tight string waiting to break. Everyone thought I was doing okay because that was the public mask I wore to hide my sadness. I looked fine on the outside, but I was a living hell on the inside. People thought I was strong, but I was not. I was simply trying to survive. I cried in silence as it made people uncomfortable to talk about him. I want to talk about Garrett. I want his life to matter. He is still my son, and I am still very proud of him. Even people with good intentions didn't understand my pain. They wanted me to move on and to be happy. But they have never experienced a hole in their heart like that. There are days that I questioned whether I wanted to be here or not, but I know that is not what Garrett would want for me. I had to make a choice. I could crawl in a black hole, or I can take a step towards healing and find a way to honor Garrett and keep his legacy alive.

One key turning point for me came two years after Garrett died. A producer named Jennifer Steinman invited me to be part of an extraordinary documentary called *Motherland.* The project chronicled several mothers who had lost a child as they journeyed to South Africa in search of hope and healing. There, we came together in our brokenness and bonded as we worked with kids who showed us a perspective of human triumph and life-changing love. I went halfway around the world to understand that giving can bring healing. It was such a relief to be with other mothers for seventeen days who knew how I felt, and I didn't have to pretend or be strong.

I realized that by sharing Garrett's story, if it could help save one life, then it was worth the pain I have had to endure. I started getting invites to talk with teenagers, parents, schools, clergy, and many other groups of people about the dangers of drunk driving and making good choices. As hard as it is to talk about and relive that fateful day over and over again, it helps me see that his life was not in vain. His life still has meaning and purpose. Garrett's life is now saving other lives. I see it every day.

Don't ever take anyone or anything for granted. Everything can change in a split second. My life will never be the same. Not only did the drunk driver kill my son, he killed a part of me. Each day, I learn to live and breathe. I feel like I'm sitting on a fence. On one side is the big black hole I can fall back into; the other side is the peaceful and hopeful side with beautiful yellow sunflowers. Sometimes, I teeter and am not sure which direction I'm going to lean. I've learned that it's okay to feel that way, but each day is a choice.

I never asked to join this club, but I was given a lifetime membership when the driver chose to drink alcohol, get into his car, and kill my son. He chose to do that. Garrett did not choose to die. I didn't choose to lose my son. But I have a choice about how I face the pain of losing him. I have a choice about how I can keep his legacy alive and continue to honor him.

In Loving Memory
Michael "Garrett" Parnell
1/4/1985—2/26/2004

Debbi Rath lives in Northern California and continues to speak to audiences and share Garrett's story. She enjoys spending time with her daughter, Merissa, and her grandkids. She can be reached by email: djb16angel@yahoo.com. For information on Motherland. the documentary, please visit http://www. motherland-thefilm.org

The Next Generation
By Cecilia DiNunno

I think one of the reasons you pick out a particular new car is because you've never seen one quite like it before. Then, as soon as you drive it off the lot, you spot your unique car everywhere.

I didn't know that heroin was making a comeback and killing our children all across this country until after my daughter died. Now it seems every headline since then has had to do with the plague of death that heroin has become. It's not that the thought of Elizabeth dying hadn't crossed my mind. She used drugs, she hung around with dangerous people, and she had been in and out of jail. But I always hoped she would get to the other side and stay clean and recover. I never thought that this day would be her last, and that this drug would be the reason.

We had lived far apart for three years, she in Illinois and me in Florida, but I talked to her every day. Over the years I had tried everything: yelling, crying, reasoning, explaining, helping, not helping. She would be clean for a while—you could hear it in her voice—and I know she wanted to. I knew she was trying, but it wasn't easy for her.

What I thought and what I hoped were that the two best reasons for her to fight through this were named Kendra and Dylan. Elizabeth lived with us here in Florida nine years ago when Kendra was newborn and two years later when Dylan came.

She got her GED and was learning how to be a mom, carving pumpkins on Halloween and finding joy in taking care of the kids day to day. But after a while, bad habits slipped back in. One night there was a big fight over something stolen, and the police showed up. The next day, she packed the kids up with a boyfriend and headed up north.

I love my daughter, and I love my grandchildren. But I knew what my daughter was going through was not good for the kids. And I was right. I felt so strongly that I left my job, my house, and my husband behind to go up and try to help her any way I could, but things weren't good.

Eventually DCF stepped in and the kids ended up in foster care, thank God with a wonderful foster parent family. But I had to get those kids with me. I needed to make sure that they were safe all the time, and they could grow up with some sense of normalcy and family. I made it my mission in life, and nothing was going to stop me. It broke my heart, but if I couldn't save Liz, I could at least protect her children.

My husband and I became foster parents ourselves in order to satisfy the requirements of an Interstate Compact to get the children with us. After two years of classes and paperwork, phone calls and fingerprints, the kids finally arrived back with us.

I know Elizabeth knew it was best for the kids. We would bring them back to Illinois for visits sometimes, and though there were tearful goodbyes, she knew in her heart that her children were being taken care of. And that's the most important thing.

When I got the call from her boyfriend saying that Liz was gone, my knees buckled, my heart stopped, and my head was swimming. It's a shock and a disbelief that you can't comprehend unless you've been through it. No one can understand the hole left inside you that will always be there—every day. Time may heal some wounds, but not this one.

I can find my saving grace, though. I can make it through the day now, because of the two she left me to care for. I will still cry sometimes at the mere wisp of the thought of what I lost. She was my child—my youngest and my only girl. But my new girl, especially, who is the spitting image of her mom, with the same spirit and is smarter than all of us, for some reason, helps to fill up my heart so that the pain subsides. And her brother, who teases her to no end, has the dimples to prove his connection, and loves to make us laugh, fills it up even more.

I don't know what your saving grace is or will be, but there is something or someone out there who needs you and needs to help you heal your heart. We found it through our own grandchildren, but we also got an unexpected blessing on the side.

We thought that since we had to get our foster license in order to get our grandkids full time, we would occasionally do respite care—temporary care for kids in the foster care system for a day or two, maybe over a weekend.

On September 22, 2014 (just eight days before Elizabeth's birthday), a two-day-old infant came into our lives. Now, her little smile warms our heart every morning and all through the day. Although it's complicated, we've decided that this little lady would fit perfectly into our family and hope that we can provide her with a permanent and stable home.

It is difficult to cope and would be easy to curl up in a ball and disconnect. But if you can give yourself a reason, not so much as a distraction but as a way to make some sense of things, and pick yourself up long enough to search for that reason—foster parenting, reading to children, helping the homeless, whatever type of volunteering calls to you, or whatever path onto which you can channel some emotion—do it. The hurt will always be there, but maybe the joy you find will shine bright enough to help you find your smile again.

Additional Resources
For more information on foster parenting:
http://nfpaonline.org/
http://fostercare.com/
For information on heroin addiction:
http://www.smartrecovery.org/addiction/heroin.html
https://www.ncadd.org/

Cecilia DiNunno (friends call her CC) has four children: three boys and her youngest daughter, Elizabeth, whom she lost April, 2015. CC and her husband Chris have nine grandchildren between them. They've lived in Florida since the 1980s. She finds comfort in caring for Elizabeth's two children. CC can be reached via email: fishchef@hotmail.com

When Can I Go Home?
By Mary Johnson

The nurse had settled Cathy between the cool, fresh sheets; the orderly was setting up the oxygen tent. Soon the hissing of the life-sustaining gas began. The dusky color eased slowly from Cathy's face. A pale flush replaced it.

Cathy's doll, practically bald from being loved for two years, slept peacefully by her side. It was a birthday present from Grandma on her second birthday, and it hadn't left her side since. It was on the couch with her when we scooped her up and brought her to the hospital.

Our daughter, Cathy, had become ill the day before, but she hadn't responded to the medicine the doctor had given her. In the last few hours her breathing had become labored, and the doctor had advised getting her to the hospital where oxygen could be administered.

The nurse came back to take Cathy's temperature, but before the thermometer was stuck into her mouth, she looked first at her daddy and then at me. Smiling a weak but brave smile, she asked, "When can I go home?"

"When you're well, Sugar," I answered.

"Tell me a story, Momma," she said when the nurse was through. She seemed to be trying to bring some familiar element into the sterile atmosphere.

I went over close to her and told her a story about a kitty and a dog and their escapades frolicking about in the mud. We had given them names over the years, Fluffy and Spot. Fluffy and Spot had many adventures and misadventures, and Cathy never seemed to tire of hearing about them.

I saw the nurse coming back with a pan, and I ended my story. "Her temperature is high," she said. "I want to sponge her with this alcohol solution."

While the nurse sponged, I went back to the chair beside Paul. We sat feeling useless and helpless. Cathy, the brave one, kept throwing smiles to us from under the blurry tent. Cathy, the brave one, who could climb the tall tree in our front yard to the top and leave onlookers breathless. Cathy, the brave one, who had gotten up before her daddy and me one morning and had been discovered by us out on the driveway rollerskating.

"Honey, why are you out skating so early?" I had asked.

"Because Teresa was skating yesterday and broke her arm, and she got a new dollhouse," was the child-logical reply.

Now Cathy, the brave one, seemed to be trying to console her less-than-brave parents.

Soon the doctor arrived, ordered X-rays, and confirmed the diagnosis. "She has a very resistant form of pneumonia," he told us. "I am having the lab do a culture for us. We do occasionally run into a stubborn strain of bacteria that doesn't respond well to our drugs. The next twelve hours will be crucial."

Paul called our pastor, and he came to be with us. He comforted us with Scripture and prayer, and we began our vigil.

Needles were stuck in Cathy's arms and ankles, so the powerful antibiotics could begin to do their work. Cathy didn't flinch or cry, but she wanted me nearby to tell her more about Fluffy and Spot. With my head under her tent, we took Fluffy and Spot on a trip to the toy store, into a forest, and even rollerskating. She smiled when she thought of a kitty rollerskating.

When the aide brought Cathy's supper tray, I tried to tempt her with a spoonful of chocolate pudding, but she wasn't interested. She began to drift off to sleep, but she jerked awake soon in the strangeness of the situation. Her voice was weak now. Breathing was an effort, but she managed to ask, "When can I go home?"

I struggled to keep back my tears. "When you're well, we'll go home," I replied.

Paul, sensing my fatigue and strain, came over and said, "Let me stay with her awhile. You can walk outside and get some fresh air."

The night was beautiful and clear, and the sky sparkled with stars. It seemed unreal that under that lovely sky was a hospital, and inside that hospital was a critically ill little girl who wanted desperately to go home. Somehow the whole thing seemed detached from the beauty of the nighttime sky.

I remembered an illustration someone had given about God's will. They had said that God, from his vantage point, could see his whole beautiful plan unfolding like a brilliant tapestry, each event taking its place in the pattern to form a unified whole. From our earthly point of view we see only the underside of the tapestry, the knots and tangled threads.

I thought as I looked up into the sky, "Is the Master Weaver at work even now, fitting all this into his plan?" I felt a peace, an assurance from within, that indeed He was.

When I stepped back inside the corridor, Paul met me before I had taken many steps. I wondered briefly why he had left Cathy alone. Before I had a chance to ask, he said, "We've run into some trouble. They are doing an emergency tracheotomy in the room. They said that because of the danger of further infection we should stay out while they are operating."

I never again saw Cathy alive.

We waited in the cool, white hall and watched doctors and nurses scurry in and out of her room. Finally, Cathy's doctor came into the hall, and with tears in his eyes, put his sensitive hand on Paul's big shoulder. "We did all we could."

Our pastor was still there. One of the nurses had handed him the doll from Cathy's side, and he awkwardly thrust it toward me. Turning to Paul, he said, "I'll drive you home." Cathy had wanted so much to go home. During the drive, in my numbness and grief and tears, her words came back to haunt me. With the beloved, nearly-bald doll cradled in my arms, I stared through my tears into the star-studded sky and thought, "Cathy, dear, you are home, and someday we'll join you."

> **Mary Johnson** received her doctorate from The University of New Mexico. Her recently-published book, *A Caregiver's Guide: Insights into the Later Years*, is available at www.maryajohnsonphd.com. She is a licensed counselor in both New Mexico and Oregon, and practices in Albuquerque, NM, specializing in grief and loss.

The Michael Tree
By Clara Hinton

Never have I heard moans coming from anyone as I heard coming from deep within my soul on the evening of May 22nd. The sounds were not human. I remember choking and screaming, "No! No! No!" over and over again until I finally let go of the phone, dropping it to the floor and screaming, "God, I want to die! Please. I want to die now!"

Just two hours before, life was normal. It was a balmy spring evening spent with friends. We went to dinner, as we usually do on Friday nights. Since it was nearing Memorial Day, my friends asked if I minded riding to the cemetery as they placed some yellow roses on the gravesite of their son, who died at age five due to complications from a very common surgery. This was their ritual for the past forty years, and, of course, I said I would gladly ride along. As they got out of the car, I told them I would stay behind giving them their private time.

While sitting in the car, I began looking at family pictures on my phone. Oh, how I love my children! One picture of my son Mike, in particular, kept showing up. I enlarged the picture and looked at his features. He had just turned forty-two, and this particular picture was of Mike walking his baby sister across a lovely pathway high up in the mountains on her wedding day just a few months ago. How proud I was of Mike that day as he stood by his sister taking the place of her father! I kept looking at his picture, and it spoke to me in ways I never felt before.

I always heard that life can dramatically change in seconds, and that is just what happened. I no sooner had gotten settled into my bed with a good book and relaxing cup of iced tea when my phone began ringing. I looked to see who was calling, and, instinctively, I got a chill that ran up my spine. My daughter-in-law never called me. We always corresponded by text messaging. My body stiffened as I looked at the phone; I was frozen with fear. Why was she calling me?

When I answered, I heard the voice of my daughter-in-law's mother. The words are words I will never forget. "They tried. They tried so hard for over an hour. But it didn't work. I'm so sorry. The paramedics tried so hard." That's when the screams began. "Who? Who are you talking about? Tell me! Tell me now! Oh, God! No! No! No!"

I can remember hearing her saying, "Mike," but that is all I remember while the moans from deep within continued. I know I dropped the phone. I know I fell to the floor and buried my face and instantly wanted to die. I know that I heard the words my son had died.

Mike, his wife, and children live out of state. I have a large family—eleven children in all. Most of them live nearby, and I didn't know if anyone had called them. I will forever feel horrible for the phone call I made to my daughter that evening. I was still screaming as I hit speed dial on the phone. Nothing would come out except loud, suffocating moans. I vaguely remember her screaming back, "Mom! Is somebody trying to kill you? What's wrong?"

Then I got angry. I guess this is all part of trauma and shock. I blurted out in one fast sentence, "What don't you understand? Your brother Mike is dead!" And, then I collapsed in a heap on the floor next to my bed, again begging God to let me die. There is nothing that can measure that depth of pain.

Within fifteen minutes my bedroom was filled with five of my children. They had made a call to Memphis and were told that Mike had died. None of us knew the details of what happened, and it would be days until we were able to get the facts of Mike's death by a massive heart attack.

For months life was a sad, dark blur. My heart felt like every time it beat, it was going to explode. I am certain that a person has the ability to cry literally buckets of tears. My eyes remained swollen for weeks after Mike's death.

Around October the mother in me kicked in, and I knew that with Christmas coming and a family of deeply-grieving children and grandchildren, I needed to find some way to point us in the direction of hope. Christmas was only a few weeks away— Mike's favorite time of the year. It was our standing joke for years that Christmas never began until Mike walked through the door and said, "Why are you all sitting around doing nothing? Let the party begin!"

He was the oldest of the six brothers, and the second in line of the children. He was the spirited one, I always said. Never was there a dull moment with Mike! His wife and three children adored him. They never missed one Christmas "home" in the twenty-one years that he was married. How would we ever get through our family Christmas without Mike?

I took a walk in the field at home one day, the very field that Mike loved so much. Traces of him were everywhere: carvings in trees, empty shells where he sighted in his hunting gun, bales of hay that sat around the fire pit. My tears flowed like a river as I begged God to help me think of some way to keep Mike as our family's Christmas joy leader.

"The Michael Tree" was born that day! We would have a separate Christmas tree dedicated just to Mike. On that tree each family member who wanted to participate—both young kids and old—would bring a special ornament that told a story about Mike. This would be our Christmas Eve tradition in place of doing our usual gift exchange.

Words cannot adequately tell the amount of healing The Michael Tree has given us. Every one participated, and the ornaments were as unique as Mike: a mustache, Star Wars characters, a fishing knife, a lottery ticket. . . (Oh, how I wish I could tell the story that goes with that ornament!) Each one of us took our ornament to the tree and told our story. Every story was funny—so much of Mike was with us there that night! The greatest joy for me as a mother was to see Mike's wife and his children standing before The Michael Tree, giving a thumbs up as thankful tears streamed down their eyes. We kept the spirit of Mike alive!

The Michael Tree holds a lifetime of precious memories and reminders of my first son who remains alive in my heart—not just on Christmas, but forevermore.

Clara Hinton lives in Shanksville, PA (where Flight 93 came down on 9/11) and is the author of *Silent Grief* and *Child Loss—The Heartbreak and the Hope*. For additional resources, visit her blog: www.silentgriefsupport.com

··

CHAPTER SIX

FAITH AND PRAYER

The Brave One
By Michelene Fitzgerald

While the world was prepping for the super bowl, we were preparing to take our son off of life support. How could this be? How could life continue in such a trivial way? They are going to ask you hard questions. They are going to have you make difficult decisions. I found some small comfort in knowing that God had already made those decisions. Today is not a surprise to God.

At Caleb's birth, on December 9, 2001, we were given news that I never wanted to believe. To be told by an on-call doctor who we had never met that our newborn son may not ever walk and would have significant health issues was devastating and incomprehensible. That stranger planted a seed of fear in my heart on what should have been a day of celebration. The following day when our pediatrician arrived, we chose to listen to our doctor, who would monitor our son continuously, and not the stranger. Our pediatrician confirmed that the doctor had misspoken and was inappropriate. On this day, we chose Caleb's name because it meant "brave." Pushing forward, while my emotions were not aligned with my heart, I was determined to serve and care for those I loved.

Caleb was never given a diagnosis because he did not have symptoms consistent with hydrocephalus and spina bifida, but he did meet some of the criteria. We had genetic testing done, and he did not have any markers for concern. It was frustrating not to have a firm diagnosis because I wanted to make a plan and implement some control over the chaos and fear. Doctors would treat his symptoms as needed for his entire life. He would have periodic, acute, medical procedures, and then we would return to life as we expected.

When we decided to homeschool our oldest daughter, Savannah, our extended family did not understand why we would choose this option or why Scott would resign from the Fresno Police Department to pursue his own business. Often, neither did I. I knew that God was nudging me, but I did not know why, and again I trusted without my emotions being aligned. Scott resigned on February 6, 2004, and Caleb passed away February 6, 2005. That was an unexpected, perfect gift of 365 days that we look back and can only be thankful for.

When Caleb died, most of me died. I curled up on the hospital bed with my son and held him. I held his little body in my arms and kissed his pale face while repeatedly saying, "Mommy loves you. Mommy loves you." I repeated that for the next two hours as I internally processed what was going to happen next. I was going to have to leave him there. His spirit was gone, but his body was with me. We made a pillowcase for Savannah with his feet and handprints. We made treasures from his lifeless body. On that day, others were preparing for the Super Bowl while I was holding my sweet boy for the last time.

Caleb did not allow me to control any outcome during his three years and three months of life. Six surgeries, all very routine and full of hope. The pediatrician told us the first year that he would grow into his head by the time he was two. I knew I was prepared to love and raise this boy; no matter what he faced, we could do it together. Scott's mom was a special education teacher. I had worked as an aide in a special education classroom during college, and we had the greatest support system for this boy. I felt honored that God had chosen us to parent Caleb, and he would have a great and full life. That seed of fear never made its way deep into the soil of my heart because I chose to trust; I knew that all of his little issues passed through the hand of God and that everything was treatable.

After Caleb passed away, I was met with the foggy reality of the loss of my son and my pregnancy with our third child. I can't quite describe what life looked like. Scott functioned by training for a marathon and was emotionally unavailable for me while battling his grief and depression. Pregnant and afraid, I had to make the decision to take care of a growing baby en utero and six-year-old Savannah. Savannah's heartbreak was devastating. She had so many questions and such a void in her immediate daily life. I did not speak of the new pregnancy because I was in such denial and never wanted to love and lose again.

Controlling what I ate, how I exercised, and how I spent my time induced a sense of rigid control. If I could control how clean my house was, how my daughter was doing in school, I could determine the outcomes. Making hard decisions that did not align with my heart was something I became good at. I did not want to work, but I did. I did not want to be pregnant, but I was. I did not want to get out of bed, but I did. I would have to fight to feel emotion again because I felt like a robot.

Two numbing years after Caleb passed away, I gave birth to two more daughters. I was hormonal, emotional, and broken. I could only wonder what sin I had committed to deserve the punishment. I began questioning everything I believed. I needed to trust the promises in Psalms to keep me laser-focused on raising three girls, or I was going to derail. All I wanted was to hold my son.

I began running to worship music where I could really grapple with my salvation and emotions. My mind knew the Bible was true, but I could not tolerate what felt like God's betrayal. Why did Caleb not receive healing? On my runs I would often stop, sit on a curb, and sob. It was a protected time to be alone when no one would interrupt me because I had a toddler, a newborn, and a desperately-grieving six-year-old, Savannah. I stuffed much of my desperation unless I was out running.

When Caleb died, I emotionally died. Full of fear during both pregnancies, I tried not to burden my grieving family. The next several years were very dark for my husband and me, but I put on a marginal smile and tried to hide my devastation from our three daughters as I tried to manage this misery. The false radiance was small shoots of hope trying to burst through dead and dry soil. It all withered and did not last.

In my heart was deep joy and tragic grief dancing together. Trying to find each and make space for both in my life, I had to find a way to allow these two emotions to live as one, to coexist. I could not deny one without honoring the other, and that was going to take a deliberate act of my faith.

I held tightly to my mentor's favorite verse, Psalms 121, as she was losing her battle with cancer. She walked closely with me in the early months after losing Caleb and pointed me to Jesus, despite circumstance and emotion. The verses I allowed to be planted deep into more-prepared soil are these:

Psalm 16:8 "I have set the LORD always before me. Because he is at my right hand I will not be shaken."

Psalm 23:2-3 "He makes me lie down in green pastures, he leads me beside still waters, and he restores my soul."

Psalm 27:5 "For in the day of trouble he will keep me safe in his dwelling."

From 2009 to 2012, I was able to begin to dance with my emotions from a raw place. Pressing into running and grappling with the word of God challenged me to listen to God and really to no one else. People tried their best, but human words hurt me. There was nothing anyone could say that made my wound any better. Listening to people made me angry. I had just lost my dad four years prior to Caleb passing away, and my heart could not take the world. My hope was in Heaven and that was all that felt secure.

"The Lord your God is with you, the Mighty Warrior who saves. He will take great delight in you; in his love he will no longer rebuke you, but will rejoice over you with singing." Zephaniah 3:17

In 2012 I began to allow myself back into relationships. After losing Caleb, I didn't really have the ability to be superficial with people. For my family, life became deep, authentic, and fairly incapable of insignificant daily chatter. Seven years into the grief, I knew that my story had a voice, and others needed to hear it. I have been able to speak to women's groups and journey with a couple of moms who have buried children. It is a group that is safer together, and I was willing to be vulnerable again. We won't know redemption until Heaven. I knew the Lord would renew my strength; He was my revival, and I would wait for His healing.

Michelene Fitzgerald resides in Fresno, CA with her husband of twenty years and three daughters. She continues to work with homeschooling families through California Virtual Academies (CAVA) and is in her seventeenth year of teaching. Michelene blogs at fitzcrewfresno.blogspot.com and spends much of her free time running, cheering for her girls on the pool deck, and cooking. Each year her family hosts a book drive for Caleb's friends at Exceptional Parenting Unlimited (https://www. epuchildren.org/). To date, they have donated 1, 200 books in Caleb's name. Michelene can be reached at fitzcrew@gmail.com

Lost and Found
By Eddie Rivera

It all started in high school when my girlfriend got pregnant during our senior year. We were only seventeen years old. Most kids were focused on graduation and which college they wanted to go to. Even though we had been high school sweethearts for years, we were young and scared. We lived in a small, very conservative town. I always wondered what would people think of us?

After high school, I had plans to go into the military and wanted my girlfriend to come with me, get married, and start our family. I knew if I could get through boot camp, then it would give me an income to support her. We could start our lives away from the glare of a small town. Instead, when I had been in the military for a few months, her family convinced her that the best option was to give our child up for adoption. Her father did not really accept the relationship since we were from two different races. We lived in a very segregated town where there were very defined social and ethnic groups. My mom tried to convince her and her parents to allow us to raise the baby and that she would help. Instead, they gave him up for adoption without my knowledge or consent.

By January, 1989, I had entered into a new world: the military. I had to secure my future. After a few months, I went back home and met with the birth mom and saw photos of our son. She said, "Sometimes you have to love someone enough to let them go." That day, I had to let both of them go as I knew there was no future with either of them. After that, I was ordered to move to Japan with the military, where I would live for several years. I ended up in the Persian Gulf in the middle of the Persian Gulf War. It was probably one of the scariest, but most honorable, times of my life.

With the turmoil and uncertainty of my past, I knew that I wanted my life to be stable, so I threw myself into my military career. I had been keeping in touch with another woman I knew from high school. When I got home on leave, she and I connected and spent some quality time together, getting to know one another. Somehow or another, I convinced her to drive with me to California in the first new car I had ever bought. Thinking that we would settle down a bit and see where life would take us, when I checked into the base in California, I quickly found out that they would be sending me back to war. After a long six months of continued war, I finally returned home. My girlfriend and my car were still there, so that was a good sign; I did the next best thing and married her. She has been my wife for twenty-three years.

Many years went by, and I continued to have a successful military career and a great marriage. We started our own family and had two daughters. I counted the years until my son turned eighteen. This was the age that I thought he would be curious enough to come looking for me. I was determined to reconnect with him; each face I saw in a crowd always left me curious. This was before the Internet, and research and resources were not readily available. Still, I researched heavily, looked for any information I could find, and prayed earnestly to find him. I knew the only way I would be able to locate him was to track down my old girlfriend. It was almost an obsession and was starting to put a strain on my family and my life, but I had to do it.

After making multiple calls to nearby cities and counties, I was about to give up. I said a little prayer and asked for God to please put her in my life. I said I would make only one more phone call. When I called, a man answered and said, "Honey, you have an old friend on the phone." She said, "I knew this day would come; I just didn't know when." I told her I was on a mission to find our son. At first she was reluctant to give me any information that I wanted in regards to my son, but eventually she gave me the information I needed: his name and where he was given up for adoption.

I called the place and said I have a package for him and wanted to confirm the address. This was a closed adoption, and they don't give that information up to anyone, but the woman on the phone was distracted and gave me the address. That was another God moment—that was all I needed.

My heart was racing and my fingers were shaking as I sent a letter to his adoptive parents with my contact info. He was seventeen and a senior in high school. How ironic that he was the same age I was when his life started! They sent me a letter back saying that they were happy to hear from me. They had adopted two kids and had promised each to help them find their birth parents once they were eighteen. They left my letter on their kitchen counter, and Charley (my son) found it.

Every day, I would get a call with a hang-up from a blocked number around the same time. Finally, it dawned on me that it had to be my son calling. So when the calls came in, I started talking into the phone with encouraging things even when he didn't say anything back. This went on for several months. Finally, I got a call from an unblocked number and answered it. His young voice was hesitant and said, "Hey, how are you?" That was the first time I ever heard my son's voice! I had been waiting nearly eighteen years for that sound; it was a magical moment for me. I couldn't believe that after all these years, my dreams were starting to come true.

He was very curious to meet me, so after he graduated from high school, I flew him to Seattle and we had an amazing time. It was everything I dreamed of. We built a great relationship and continued to talk to each other on a regular basis for years. He fit in seamlessly as part of our family. My wife just thought the world of him. He was able to connect with his mother as well. He and I were very close. I watched him graduate from college. He wanted to be a firefighter.

In his mid-twenties, he met a girl at church and fell in love. Eventually, they got married and had a little girl. I was thrilled to be there to share some of the lifelong dreams I had for my son when he was born, especially after missing his first eighteen years.

Charley was working as a welder. He got hurt at work, and the doctor gave him a prescription for an opiate to help with the pain. After he finished that prescription, he realized he was addicted to it. He called and told me that he needed to take care of it and that he was going to disappear for a little bit. He found a facility, checked himself into rehab, and began his recovery from prescription drug addiction. We were impressed at how well he handled it and was making the effort to wean himself off the medication. After all, this was not an illegal drug. It was a prescription medication. How harmful could it be? Then, as soon as he got home, he relapsed. So he checked himself into another place and went through the process again. By now, he was starting to lose hope that he would be able to stop the medication. He didn't like the shame or stigma of being called an "addict," but always faced it head on.

We had many conversations about the battles of the mind, addiction, and very personal struggles. I was happy to be his confidante. He always reached out when he needed help.

We spoke several times per week; Charley would share his fears, doubts, and struggles. He felt like he had failed his family and his wife. He worked so hard on himself, yet he had so much shame that he could not seem to beat this. He had been a good student, graduated from high school and college, and was raised in the church. He had a loving and supportive family. He would share how the drugs had really played tricks on his mind, even long after he had stopped taking them. It was as if they had somehow warped his sense of cognitive thinking, some residual and long-term effect. He had a hard time trusting himself. He decided to go into a sober living facility.

He called me on a Saturday to check in, and we talked briefly. On Sunday, he went to church with his adoptive mother and father; the sermon was on addictions. He went to lunch with his parents, and then went back to the sober living place.

That afternoon, Charley made the decision that his struggle was too much. He lost the battle of the mind and took his own life. He sent his mom a text to say goodbye and where to find him. He hung himself on a tree at the lake, the same lake where he always said he felt peace and truly was himself.

I couldn't believe that he lost all hope, even with all the support. I never expected it and always believed that he would be able to beat this addiction. How could I have prevented it? At that moment, I understood that people who commit suicide are not trying to escape their friends or family; they are trying to escape themselves. The pressure and the hopelessness that seems external is really such a harsh internal battle of the mind.

There are many people who threaten to commit suicide, and often, they are not the ones who actually do it. The sad truth is that there is often no real warning when someone is suffering so much. The person who quietly whispers, "I don't know if I can go on," is the one you need to worry about. That is the person you need to keep an eye on full time. Move in with them. Keep them close. Watch them at all times. Encourage them to get help. It was a very subtle comment, but I never fully understood how much weight it carried. I never dreamed he would ever take his own life, especially when he had a beautiful daughter who needed him.

Nothing in this life is worth living for more than your own children. Live for them. I personally had never known anyone who had committed suicide before. It was easy for me to judge others from the outside, but now it had happened to my family.

I can never fill that void of missing Charley, but I am so grateful that we developed the strong relationship that we had. The greatest gift was the miracle of connecting again with my son. I didn't focus on the years we lost, only on the time we had together.

I realized that God was with me in that journey to find Charley. He was with me at his funeral. He is still with me now in my pain. My faith in God gives me hope that I will see Charley again someday. I know he is in a better place where he is not suffering. The journey for me is that the battle of my own mind continues now with losing him. I know that I have to be here for my family and must take care of myself.

At his funeral, I looked around and saw the hurt in all of his family and friends, including his birth mother and myself. I knew that we all felt some guilt as if, somehow, we had been responsible for his actions. However, I know that it was ultimately his choice to take his own life. I also know as sad as I feel, his birth mother had to feel worse. She gave birth to him. I prayed for God to take that pain away from her. I prayed that others would learn from his death and also see the pain that resonates within the family left behind. I prayed that Charley's life would inspire others to choose to get the help they need—that they would choose life.

I'm writing these words only two months after we lost Charley. My wounds are still fresh, and I'm emotionally raw, but I make the conscious choice every day to keep living and keep loving—for Charley.

Eddie Rivera lives in Oregon with his wife and two daughters. He strives to create a relationship with his grand daughter and Charley's adopted family. He can be reached via email at: eariver1@gmail.com

Just for Today
By Karen Tesi

I glanced through my son Jacob's Alcoholics Anonymous book and noticed something he had written on the inside cover. The words written were, "Just for Today."

I recalled when he was going to AA meetings. There were times he had attended two or three times a day. I thought it was such a waste of time. It made absolutely no sense to me. I did not understand because I was not an addict.

Death is a thief that stole my loved one away. Within a split second, life as I knew it was over. I didn't get a chance to say goodbye, nor did I get the opportunity to prepare myself for the inevitable. On November 24, 2009, my son, Jacob, died unexpectedly of a drug overdose. After a ten-year roller coaster ride of sobriety and non-sobriety, he had come home for the Thanksgiving holiday and didn't share with me that he was, once again, struggling.

As I tried to think of a future without my son, I became consumed with horror. An overwhelming urge to take off running like Forrest Gump came over me. Run, Karen, run!

I could see how very easy it would've been to slip into insanity from grief and never come out of it. This was a fight I never thought I would have to engage in. Each day had enough difficulty in it that it was impossible for me to even think about tomorrow. In fact, I dreaded "tomorrow" because I knew that, for the time being, it would be more of the same.

As the first few days turned into weeks, I began to adopt the words that Jacob had written, "Just For Today." You see... I, too, needed to exist in each day that went by, being present only for the moment that I happened to be in. Yes, in order to survive, I had to live day by day, hour by hour, and in the early stages, moment by moment. Had there been a support group that I could have attended, I would have been there not only upwards of three times a day, but perhaps I might have pitched a tent and camped out in the parking lot of the meeting facility. But, there was no such place to go in the city where I lived. I called a local hospital to inquire about their grief support groups only to be told that I had to wait a minimum of ninety days after the loss to attend their program. I could not wait ninety days. I needed immediate assistance.

Although I was a worship leader and enrolled in Bible College at the time of my son's death, I needed answers. I needed to know that Jacob was all right. I needed to know that I was going to be all right. I wanted to know if there really was a God that I could count on. My faith in God and all that I had believed up to that point was shaken.

My friends did their best to encourage me; even a therapist with a specialty in grief treatment tried to counsel me. Week after week I sat sobbing in her office, saying the same things and getting nowhere. Even though she was kind and supportive, nothing seemed to help. I needed something more. It was in this state of emotional urgency that I began to search the scriptures with a voracity as never before. I read page after page and began to journal. I had never kept a journal before; it seemed silly to me. Yet, some days I would sit and journal for hours.

The more I read and searched for comfort, the more I learned and became convinced that NOTHING could separate me or Jacob from the love of God (Romans 8:38). I read about promises and a hope for the future in Jeremiah 29:11. I read about the good shepherd who would leave the ninety-nine sheep on the hill just to go and find the one that wandered off and became lost in Matthew 18:12. I read the book of Psalms, which was loaded with encouraging words about a forgiving, delivering, restoring, healing, and rescuing God. It was this God who in time rescued me from the dark place in which I had been living. And it is this God who can and is willing to reach down from His throne and pull any and all grieving parents out of a pit of despair. As I read these scriptures and many like them, a transformation was taking place inside of me.

I'm reminded of the Biblical story of the Exodus, when the Israelites were in the wilderness. The story tells us that God gave provision for them every day. The Hebrew word for the food he gave them is *Man* or *Manna*, meaning, *what is it?* Whatever it was, they would gather it every morning, and it was their sustenance for the day. If they tried to gather more than a day's supply, it would rot by the next day. There was only one specific day per week when they were told to gather enough for two days.

Here we are shown just one example of how God will provide on a daily basis. God will provide for you, too. I am living, breathing, and thriving today because of a God who took my hand and walked with me through those very dark days and is still encouraging me even now as I write these words.

You are not alone. Many bereaved parents are cheering you on. Picture us encouraging you as you crawl toward the finish line in the race towards recovery. Trust me, it is a slow crawl. Those early days had many emotions in them. In the beginning stages of grief, there are many things to feel each day. Today the loneliness can be more than you can bear at times. Today the regret might be the size of a mountain that you just can't climb. However, the provision and promises of God are sufficient for us today. Will it be easy? No. In fact, recovery is the toughest journey you will ever embark on as a parent. But, you can do it!

Many years have passed since my devastating loss. God walked with me every day through the uncertainty of what lay ahead. Even though I felt isolated and alone, He was with me. Little by little, day-by-day, I became stronger. Eventually, my joy was restored. I went from wanting to lie down and die to a newfound mission in my life. I never wanted losing a child to be part of my life's story, but it is. In the last two years I have had numerous opportunities to assist other parents on their journey in recovering from the same loss you and I have suffered.

You will see your child again; this is not the end. In the meantime, your child is safe in the presence of a loving God.

Jesus said, "Do not worry about tomorrow. . . each day has enough trouble of its own." This is good advice for anyone in any time of life, especially after the death of a child. So for now, stay in today.

Karen Tesi, a licensed Messianic Minister has worn many hats. Karen is a motivational speaker who teaches Biblically-sound, topical lessons and word studies from an ancient Hebrew perspective for various churches and fellowship groups, as well. She is an accomplished vocalist and placed in the top ten finalists in the 2010 Best of the Blessed national competition. Karen's book, *My Cup of Tears,* was birthed out of an inspired plan for recovery after losing her son, Jacob. Karen resides in California and can be reached for bookings at Karen@AncientThingsMinistries.org

On a Mission
By Dale West

Our oldest daughter, Sonya, was in college. She came home one Thanksgiving and shared with us that she wanted to go to Haiti and be a missionary. She wanted the blessing of our entire family before she made the final decision. She had researched the costs of the trip, decided where she wanted to go, and found a hospital with a school and an orphanage inside of it. She knew this was where she wanted to be. She also was able to raise the money from three different churches that helped her realize that dream.

She left for her mission trip to Haiti on December 31, 1990. There was a group of us at the airport to see her off. As she waved goodbye and stepped into the jet way, we never realized that was the last time we would see her.

She was only there for a few months. She was working with orphans, feeding them, giving them physical therapy and love. These were outcasts that no one else wanted. She would volunteer to do anything, whether it was helping in the hospital operating room, comforting sick people, or making food for others. She would walk a quarter mile to make phone calls and tell us about her adventures. We couldn't wait to get these reports. This was before cell phones or the Internet, so it was a challenge to communicate with each other.

Sonya had experienced an unusually disappointing week and had decided to take a break for the weekend. So she caught a ride with three Haitian doctors who were headed back to Port-au-Prince. Along the way, a cow ran in front of the car. They dodged the cow and swerved across the road into an oncoming vehicle. All those in the car survived, except Sonya. She died May 3, 1991, just a few weeks shy of her twenty-first birthday.

I got the call late on a Friday night. Even though it was late, our house was full of people who wanted to offer their support, mostly from our church. I remember our minister looking me in the eye and saying that he knew I probably wanted answers, but he had none to give me. All he said was, "God loves you. I don't know why this happened, but God loves you and will be with you through all of this."

After Sonya died, it was another challenge to get her body back to the U.S. We tracked down the people she was staying with. The American consulate told us it would realistically take thirty days to get her body returned to us. Our church and the city of Pampa, Texas, managed to raise $25,000 within a few days from our small community of only 15,000 people. We had to hire someone to go retrieve her body and get it back to us. Between raising the money, calling Haiti, and coordinating with the consulate, we were shocked that it only took seven days. The man who put her body on the plane said he had been doing it for thirty years and never saw a body move that quickly. We also received a bill for only half of the fee. That, too, was a mystery to everyone and something they had not seen before. It was evident to me that God was working to help us, even with the most difficult tasks.

Twenty-one years later, our son, Kurt, was invited to go on a mission trip to Haiti with his church. He loved his sister so much; he had searched for years to find a woman who was like her. When he found one, he married her. His wife was pregnant, and, understandably, he did not want to go. Naturally, he was feeling some resistance and made the excuse that he didn't have the money to go, bad timing, etc. But when he prayed about it, God told him to go. He was in the middle of a big job at his work, the largest one to date. He had just completed the job, and guess what his commission was? The exact amount he needed to go on this mission.

While he was in Haiti, Kurt was doing hard jobs, like pouring concrete to help build a church. He hated it. It was hot and humid and really hard work. He really wanted to do something else. They asked him to help pray with people in the prayer line. Through an interpreter, he would pray with people who had waited in the long prayer line. He had been there a few hours when a beautiful young Haitian woman with a bright smile came up in line. Most women were very reserved and would not look you in the eye. He asked what her name was? It was Sonya. Immediately, he had the healing he had been waiting for and realized why he was there.

The next year, my other daughter, Christa, and I were invited to go on a missionary trip. They had first planned to go somewhere else, but then changed it to Haiti at the last minute. Christa felt that it was a sign. Now this was twenty-two years after Sonya died. I didn't think I could do it. Just like my son, I fought it and talked myself out of going. But when I prayed about it, I felt a resounding peace that it was something I needed to do for my own healing.

When we landed, I imagined how Sonya must have felt when she arrived. I felt the hot sun on my face and deeply breathed in the air of Haiti. I saw how peaceful and loving the people were. We went to the hospital with the orphanage where Sonya had worked. We saw where she had lived, where she ate, where she slept, and literally followed in her footsteps.

We asked the interpreter if anyone had been there for a long time. We actually found a woman there who remembered Sonya. When we asked about our daughter, her face lit up and she said, "Oh yes, Sonya. She loved everybody." That is when I knew her legacy was living on, even all those years later.

On the twentieth anniversary of her death, I was sitting in my recliner and was reflecting on Sonya and her journey. The phone rang, and a young man asked if I had a daughter named Sonya. He had searched my name online and somehow tracked me down. He said, "I need to tell you about your daughter. She was an upper classman when I was a freshman. She took me under her wing and gave me counseling. She was so open and helpful. She prayed with me and for me, and would talk to me for hours. She helped me through so much. She even wrote me letters from Haiti. I was devastated when I heard that she had died. I have two kids who are nine and eleven. They told me they wanted to go on a mission trip with their church. And when I asked them where, they said Haiti. I immediately thought about Sonya. I went through my closet and found an old shoebox with letters from Sonya and read them with my kids. I told them that this is what a true missionary sounds like." And then he asked me if I would like the letters. Within a few days, he sent these amazing letters, full of Sonya's spirit and personality, that I had never seen before. It was like having a piece of her back after so many years.

If you are a believer, there are a thousand things that are worse than death—even the death of your own child. The worse thing that can happen is to lose a child without faith. Then, there is no hope. I have some comfort knowing that Sonya was serving God when she died. She had been called there for a reason. When I went to visit Haiti, I could still see her mission at work, over twenty years later. It gave me peace to understand that her death was not in vain.

I found the following scripture to be comforting, even after all these years:

"Good people pass away; the godly often die before their time. But no one seems to care or wonder why. No one seems to understand that God is protecting them from the evil to come. For those who follow godly paths will rest in peace when they die."
—Isaiah 57:1-2 NLT

> **Dale West** lives in Pampa, Texas with his wife, Bobbie. He can be reached at 1946dwest@gmail.com

My Friends Need Jesus
By Cindy Brown

In March, 2011, Spring Break came early. The high school put on a Spring Fling Festival the Friday before with games, challenges, snacks, and live music put on by students. Our son,

Joshua (JB to friends), was very excited because the principal was allowing him to participate even though he had graduated a semester earlier.

He had just written two songs about two weeks prior to the festival and was eager to share them. One was about the Holy Spirit, titled "Waterfall," and the other one was about Christians not doing what they were called to do and titled "One Man Running." He and his band were so nervous because they had never played for the public before. They had a few mishaps; however, considering this was their first time to perform, they did very well.

Later that weekend, he went to Austin for a few days to visit just about everyone he ever knew growing up because that next week he was going to San Antonio to join the Navy.

The Timeline

On the Wednesday of Spring Break, Josh was back home from Austin and studying for his Armed Services Vocational Aptitude Battery (ASVAB). He took a break to write a song titled "Save Me from Myself." When I got home from work, he couldn't wait to sing it for me. I told him it sounded like a cry out to Jesus, which sparked a deep conversation. Just eight months prior, in July of 2010, Joshua had a bad bout with rebellion just after he turned eighteen, deciding to move out so he could do his own thing and experiment with drugs. Fortunately, this was short lived, and he came home six weeks later. Little did I know, our conversation would become the backdrop for the rest of my life.

We talked about his walk with Jesus, and he shared how he didn't tell many people he was a Christian because he felt he wasn't a very good one. I told him that humility was what made him a good one. He talked about his friends and how they desperately needed Jesus and wondered what it would take to reach them. His heart was deeply burdened for them, especially since he was leaving for the Navy. He shared how great his testimony was going to be one day because of all the things he had experienced and how he would be able to relate to anyone. That night his dad, Michael, taught him basic electronics in a couple of hours to help him with the ASVAB. Josh was a fast learner when he applied himself.

The next day, Thursday, Michael drove him into Austin to the Navy recruiter and put him on a van to San Antonio. Josh was so nervous about the ASVAB and whether or not he would do well enough to get the nuclear program he wanted.

Friday afternoon, Josh called Michael to tell him he made an 85% on the ASVAB and that he was offered the nuclear program. He was so excited and proud; they just needed him to send in more info on his health history. Michael told him how very proud we were of him and how far he had come. That night Josh came back to Burnet to spend the last weekend of Spring Break with his friends.

On Saturday he sent me a text stating he was worried that his health history wouldn't be good enough. I told him, "God is in control; just trust Him." He said he trusted Him and that he loved me. That is the last time I spoke to him.

Sunday morning, March 20th (the first day of spring), Josh and his friend decided to go to Llano to help a mutual friend who had been arrested for unpaid tickets. The boys had a reputation of taking care of people, making sure everyone was included and having each other's back in times of crisis. This time was no different except the inclusion part. A third person wanted to go with them, and Joshua looked him in the eye and said, "You can't go with us this time." That phrase stood out because that wasn't something he said very often, especially to this person. So the two boys got a snack around 3 a.m. and headed off to Llano, using the back roads.

Jordan, our daughter, and I usually went to church early Sunday mornings while my husband would pick up my brother and meet us there later when church started. This Sunday morning Michael was late. I picked up my phone to call and check on him and saw a text from one of Josh's friends. She was asking how Josh was, that she heard he had been in an accident. I gathered my things, got Jordan, and went out into the foyer to call Michael, but he didn't pick up. I paced frantically waiting for him to get to church or pick up the phone, thinking we have to hurry and get to the hospital or something. I looked up and saw Michael drive up, but my brother wasn't in the car with him.

I told Jordan to stay there and went out to the car to tell him Josh might have been in an accident. The look on Michael's face when he got out of the car said it all. It was the same look he had given me when he told me my mother had died eleven years earlier. Our worst fears had been realized. Josh and his friend had died in a tragic accident. Michael said he was about to pick up my brother when a sheriff drove up and asked if he was Joshua Brown's father. He stated the boys were driving a 300ZX at a high speed when the driver lost control of the car and overcompensated at the fork in the road. The car rolled and hit a tree around 3:20 am on Park Road 4. Joshua was the passenger and didn't have any identification; therefore, it took a while to find out who he was.

I dropped to the ground as my heart broke into a million pieces and the words that came out of my mouth even shocked me. I said, "God will be glorified in this; let there be salvation for every tear." These weren't my words. They were promises from God that He would bring beauty from ashes.

Wednesday, March 23, were the funerals for both boys. That morning Michael left me at home to take Jordan up to the church early. She thought she might want to sing at the funeral to honor her brother, but later just couldn't bring herself to do so. I was on the couch in the most physical pain I had ever felt in my life. I thought I would be dead by the time Michael got back to the house. I fell to my face on the floor moaning, trying to cry out, but no words would form. I actually couldn't speak; it just came out in groans. Finally, I screamed, "God, I need to know where my son is! I can't bear this; it is going to kill me!"

In the background, I heard music and realized Michael had left the TV on tuned into a radio station. I got onto my knees as I listened to the words, *"I've got my memories Always inside of me, but I can't go back, back to how it was."* The lyrics made me ask God, "Is this for me?" and the song filled the room as if Joshua were singing it himself. . . *"This is home, now I'm finally where I belong."* I wondered who the artist was, and when I got closer to the TV, I saw the song was called, "This Is Home" by Switchfoot. This happened to be the theme song from one of Joshua's all time favorite book series, *Chronicles of Narnia.* After that, I was able to get up, get dressed, and go to my 18 ½ year old son's funeral knowing, without a doubt, he was home with Jesus. God empowered me to speak at the funeral. I don't remember all that was said, but I will never forget that fifty of his friends asked Jesus into their hearts that day. That was the day I became Mama Brown.

The Journey

The road ahead of us had its ups and downs, but God was faithful every step of the way. He used moments from those last few months with Josh that didn't seem special at the time to press us forward and speak life into us as we grieved. He showed us how Joshua, by visiting all his friends and singing at the school after he had already graduated, had primed hearts to receive God's message of hope through Jesus at the funeral. I learned that nothing is wasted and, if you let Him, God can bring beauty from ashes. During this time, music spoke deeply to us; it felt like God wrote a new song for us with every new stage of grief we came across. I expected God to speak to me whereever I was or whatever I was doing. He promised that He would turn my mourning into joy, and I was looking for it.

One way He spoke to me was through one of Joshua's favorite songs, "In the Light" by DC Talk. This song was special to Josh because it was his testimony. He used it to tell people how he was *"still a man in need of a savior"* and that all he wanted was *"to be in the light as He is in the light."* DC Talk hasn't been a group since 2000, however, that song played on the Christian radio station every time I got in the car for thirty days starting the day Josh died. I delved deep into God's word looking for answers and kept going back to Hebrews 11, the faith Hall of Fame chapter. All the people mentioned died in hope of the promise, but never attaining it here, in hope of a better resurrection. Joshua's friends finding the truth in Jesus would definitely give him a better resurrection.

At the first anniversary of his going home, I asked Michael how we should honor Josh's memory. He said that Josh himself told me when he said, "Mom, my friends need Jesus." So we committed to share the hope of Jesus Christ with his friends, who happened to be anyone he ever met. We still have moments that take our breath away and drop us to the ground, but my Jesus continually picks us up and breathes life back into us so that we may do the same for others.

It is crazy sometimes how God works. We thought Josh was going to be our legacy, but, in reality, we became his.

Psalm 62:6 "Truly He is my rock and my salvation; He is my fortress, I will not be shaken." This last verse has since become our root verse for our new business where we continue Joshua's legacy.

Cindy Brown resides in Burnet, Texas, with her husband, Michael. She has lived in Burnet with Michael and their daughter, Jordan, since June of 2009. They are the owners of

Unshakable Grounds coffee shop. The coffee house gives them an opportunity to reach out to their community and share the love of Jesus through everyday encounters. Cindy has hopes of writing a book about the amazing faithfulness of Jesus in all circumstances. You may find Cindy on Facebook at Cindy Yates Brown (MamaBrown) and Unshakable Grounds, on Twitter: @Mama_CBrown and at www.UnshakableGrounds.com

....

CHAPTER SEVEN

GIFTS FROM BEYOND

The Unexpected Gift
By Irene Freitas

In 1985 my husband and I were going through the process of divorce. We had four children—one boy and three girls. My oldest child, James Anthony Moreno II (named after my first husband), was fifteen years old. We had a very special mother/son bond. I was blessed because my son was never embarrassed to shower me with affection. James had a very warm and loving personality. His family was important to him, and he was a protective big brother to his sisters. James was incredibly smart, and he was always an athlete. He loved football, also practiced martial arts, and enjoyed boxing. Things changed once my husband moved out; James took a turn for the worse. He really struggled emotionally with the breakup of the family because he was close to his stepfather. He started spending more time out of our home with his friends, and he began experimenting with drugs and alcohol. He also started missing school.

One morning, James decided to skip school to go to the lake with his friends. I believe divine intervention inspired me to walk with him that morning. We walked to his bus stop, hugged goodbye, and told each other, "I love you." Those were the last words spoken between my son and me, and it would be the last time I ever saw, touched, or hugged him. James went missing after that. For three months, I worked with the police, trying desperately to find him. His friends lied and said they did not know where he was. Eventually, the truth came out that he had taken a recreational drug and then had gone for a swim in the lake. Although he had always been a strong swimmer, he'd lost his dexterity and sense of direction and drowned. The other teenagers he had been with were also doing drugs, and they didn't want to get caught. So they didn't tell anyone that he had drowned, myself included, nor did they admit to seeing him that day. Eventually, I would be told that they didn't help him out of fear of drowning themselves.

Upon filing a missing person's report, I was advised to contact the coroner's office. The coroner told me that they had a John Doe, believed to be in his thirties, so it couldn't have been my fifteen-year-old son. I continued to hope that he was alive somehow. Dreadfully, months later, a dental record comparison proved John Doe was actually my son, James. My son had been in the water so long that his body became completely unrecognizable. I learned the harsh way that an unclaimed body is cremated after a certain amount of time. So by the time I learned of my son's death, he had already been cremated.

My heart was shattered that he had died alone, and that I didn't get to protect him from death. I needed to honor him and say good-bye. So we buried his urn in the same cemetery where my brother, Delfino, was buried. Even though my son had been cremated, I wanted him to have a marked grave, a place where people who loved him could go remember him. At the time, I didn't know how significant that decision would be.

Despite my heartbreak over the loss of my beloved son, I still had to get through my divorce. I was a single mom, and I had to raise three other kids who desperately needed me. Tormented and lost, I knew I had to be strong for my daughters, Sonja, Yolanda, and Andrea.

My family had suffered tragedy before, and I had always considered myself to be a strong person. After all, I come from a strong mother and father. I had experienced the pain of losing siblings and relatives, but the pain of losing my son rocked me to my core. I was only able to cope because I had so much family and support. My parents had thirteen kids, and they endured the deaths of their first three children. So my mother understood my pain, and she was able to empathize with me. Prior to my son's death, my oldest sister had already experienced the loss of her first three children, so she was also a substantial source of consolation to me. My family tried their best to hold me up, and they surrounded me with so much love. My daughters also really held me together. They were young, but they were my source of inspiration to heal. Nearly twenty years after I lost my son, James, three more of my siblings lost their oldest sons. We are each others' support group, and we continue to seek solace in one another.

After the loss of my son, anytime I felt sorry for myself, I would read a story of someone who had it worse than I did. I would also think about the people who lost their only child and didn't have any others, or couldn't have any others. I would remind myself of how my mom and sister each suffered through the deaths of three kids; I felt like their pain was much worse. So I tried to reflect on my blessings, which included my three daughters. That's how I try to look at everything in life.

Soon after my son died, I met Frank, an amazing man who came into my life at the time when I needed him most. He became my rock, and he carried me through my pain. Three years later we married, and he became a stepfather to my daughters. We had our own daughter together, and we named her Jamie, in remembrance of my son, James. My nephew, Delfino, named after my deceased father and brother, also came to live with us. Having Delfino in our home brought me joy, as he was part of my brother whom I had missed and been very close to. He became like a son to Frank and me, and like a brother to my girls. So our family was expanding.

When Delfino married, he had children of his own; I fell in love with all of them. However, I became attached to his son,

Erik. My husband passed away when Erik was a just baby, but, for a short time, Frank and I called him our pretend grandson. It felt good to have boys in our home and a part of our family again. We are all still close today.

I've always tried to find ways to keep James' memory alive. I honor him on the anniversary of his death. And every year on his birthday, our extended family gets together, and I make his favorite pie and cook his favorite meal. We share stories about him all the time, even so many years later.

One year in particular, eighteen years after he had passed away, a life-altering gift was bestowed upon me. It was March 16th, James' birthday, and like every year, I went to the cemetery with my sister Rosie. As we walked to his grave, I noticed that someone had left flowers. They were purple, his favorite color. When I picked them up, there was a note. It read, "To my Dad, from your daughter, Corina." I said to my sister, "Look, they put them on the wrong grave," and we had a little chuckle about it. Then, as we started looking at the other graves, we noticed they had birthdates in the early 1900s. None of those buried there were young enough to have a daughter alive today.

When I turned the card around, there was a note that said, "Please call me." My knees buckled. What did that mean? Could it even be possible? I took the note back home, and my daughters, who were now grown, were very leery. They didn't want me to get my hopes up. Being protective of me, my oldest daughter, Sonja, decided she would call the number to speak with Corina.

My hands shook and my body trembled as I waited to hear the news. This was now 2003, eighteen years after James had passed away. The woman identified herself as Corina. She was eighteen years old, and she explained that she had recently discovered that my son was her father!

She also explained that she had a three-year-old son, and they both wanted to meet us.

We decided to meet in a public place that was neutral, so we settled on a local park. During that time, I was a teacher at a daycare center, which only exasperated my yearning for a grandchild. We didn't know for sure if she really was my son's daughter, so I knew I had to be cautious about getting my hopes up. As I sat in anticipation with my family at the picnic tables, my heart and my mind were flooded with conflicting emotions and doubts. But as soon as she stepped out of my daughter's car, I knew instantly that she was my granddaughter. She looked just like her dad. I can't even describe the overwhelming rush of emotions I experienced, while watching part of James walk back into my life, literally from the grave, eighteen years later!

In one evening, I found out I was a grandmother and also a great-grandmother. My daughters instantly became aunts. What an incredible shock! James died before he could tell any of us.

As I spoke with her (and eventually her mother), the story started to come together. Corina's mother, like my son, had been fifteen years old when she was conceived. So after James died, she married another man, and he raised Corina as his own. When Corina turned eighteen, her stepfather passed away, and, of course, Corina was very upset. It was then that her mother decided to reveal to her that James was actually her real father. She took Corina to my son's grave, and that's how Corina knew where to leave the flowers for us. And the rest is history. . .

The pain that I had been feeling all of these years was lighter. I was so thankful for the miracle of this gift in my life.

Corina's son, Anthony (my great-grandson), is such an amazing gift to me. I didn't get the opportunity to watch Corina grow up, so I am grateful that I've been able to watch Anthony grow from a toddler to an exceptional young man. I cherish the time we spend together. I once asked him, "Do you ever remember a time when you didn't know me?" He responded by saying, "I've known you my whole life, Grandma." That statement brought me joy beyond belief. I am very proud of my great-grandson. In addition to being an honest, kindhearted person, he has many talents. He enjoys playing the violin and takes interest in classical compositions. He's also an exceptional student, with a 4.0 GPA, in honors classes. And he's an athlete, just like James. Recently, Corina gave birth to a baby girl, so now I also have a great-granddaughter.

Death happens to everyone. But when it happens too soon, it is often hard for us to grasp the purpose. I still don't understand why God chose to take my son. But if James had not died, I would not have had my youngest daughter. If Corina's stepfather hadn't died, she wouldn't have known that she had a different father, and she would never have found us. If I had not insisted on a headstone for my son, she would not have had a place to bring flowers. I lost a son, but I gained a daughter, granddaughter, and great-grandchildren. And Corina gained an entire extended family that is there for her.

Sometimes, if we can allow our hearts to recognize our blessings, we can find that all the broken pieces fit together beautifully. When we try to put the pieces together from the world's perspective, it doesn't always fit. But when we look backwards, we see how people come into our lives for a bigger purpose. It's always for good. There is still a legacy left in us, even if we had an only child. That child touched and influenced others, and their legacy lives through those left behind.

The universe has a way of autocorrecting. We must embrace it even if we don't want to. We have to believe that good things will still happen and be open to that in life. I believe that one day, I will be reunited with my son, James.

In Loving Memory:
James A. Moreno II
3/16/70 - 5/28/85

Irene Freitas is a widowed devoted mother and grandmother who lives in Fresno, California. Her third husband, Frank, passed away from cancer. She still keeps in touch with Corina and also enjoys spending time with her great-grandson,

Anthony. She also has seven grandchildren, five step-grandchildren, and five step-great-grandchildren. She can be reached at: irenelinda950@gmail.com

The Gratitude Letter
By Joanie Cook

Our son Brad was diagnosed with leukemia in April, 1981, when he was eight and a half years old. Within days of his diagnosis, he was admitted to our local Children's Hospital. He underwent intensive chemotherapy for two weeks. At the end of that period, Brad was in a remission, but his battle with this disease had only begun.

Over the next two years, he received radiation treatment and chemotherapy in the form of oral medication. He handled everything remarkably well and was able to return to school within a few weeks of his initial hospitalization. After his radiation treatment, he lost his hair, but it came back, though a different color. Brad had a fraternal twin brother, Matt. They looked quite a bit alike, but after being on medication and losing his hair, Brad's appearance changed and no one had trouble telling them apart.

My husband and I were quite hopeful that Brad would stay in remission and ultimately be cured, but when Brad was fifteen and a junior in high school, the leukemia resurfaced. It was decided that the best option was to find a donor and have Brad undergo a bone marrow transplant. Matt and their younger brother, Aaron, were both tested, but Matt's blood was the best match. In fact, through all the testing prior to the transplant, the doctors were almost 100% sure that Brad and Matt were actually identical twins.

On November 22nd, the transplant was performed. It just so happened to be their sixteenth birthday! What a birthday gift—to give and receive the gift of life. When Brad was at the hospital undergoing the transplant, my husband, Rich, also donated platelets. Since then, he has continued to donate platelets every month (for twenty-six years now).

Brad and I stayed in the hospital for about six weeks, while my husband and our other two sons went back home a few hours away. By January, we were able to stay with family until Brad was cleared to go home. The next several months consisted of follow-up doctor visits and a return to school. Once again, we were quite hopeful and were so thankful that Brad was able to have the transplant. It's not always easy to find a perfect match.

In September, just a few weeks after Brad started his senior year in high school, routine blood work revealed that the cancer was back. From that point on, we talked to Brad about possibly having another transplant. He was willing, but he would need to get into a remission or at least be strong enough to withstand the treatment that would be required. He spent most of that fall and winter at the hospital, but never was able to have another transplant. His last few weeks were spent at home. He went to be with the Lord surrounded by his family and grandparents on March 2, 1990.

Through the years, people have asked us how we were able to cope with the loss of a child. It is always hard to lose a loved one, but losing a child is probably the hardest. I don't think you ever get over it. Even now, after twenty-six years, remembering what Brad and our family went through brings that sense of pain and grief back to the surface. What I can say, though, is that God has been our source of comfort and strength. I am not sure what would have happened to us without our faith to keep us going. I remember one of our pastors saying that everything we face in life has already gone before God. Nothing takes Him by surprise. Knowing that He is in control, even when we can't see the light at the end of the tunnel, sustained me through the darkest days. It's not the trials and difficulties we face in life (and no one is immune to them), but how we respond to them that is important.

I have heard that the divorce rate is very high for people who lose a child. Rich and I had been married almost twenty years when Brad died, so we had a solid foundation. Almost half of that time, we had been dealing with his illness, but we never considered separating. We made a commitment to stay together no matter what. If anything, we relied on each other for support. I can't imagine dealing with everything without my husband to share the load. We each grieved in our own way, but were able to comfort each other and never turned on each other.

Up until a month before Brad's death, I was still hoping for another transplant and feeling very anxious about everything. Then one afternoon as I was driving in town to do errands, I had this overwhelming sense of peace come over me. It is hard to explain, but I know it was God telling me to leave it in His hands. He loved Brad and had a perfect plan for his life; whether that meant He would heal him here or heal him in Heaven. It was totally out of my control. From that point on, great relief flooded over me. No matter what, it was going to be okay. A Bible verse that came to mind was John 14:27. It says, *"Peace I leave with you; my peace I give you. I do not give to you as the world gives. Do not let your hearts be troubled and do not be afraid."*

In addition to our faith in God, our family and friends were a great support. They brought food, visited Brad in the hospital, offered financial support, and comforted us in our grieving. One particular friend of ours who had lost a child to cancer a few years before came to see me at the hospital. He shared the last days of his daughter's life and the hours before her death. Just talking with him and asking him questions about what to expect made me feel less anxious.

Before his death, we encouraged Brad to write a letter to his family and friends. The following letter was read at Brad's memorial service that was attended by over 500 people, many of them from Brad's high school.

March 1, 1990

Dear Friends and Loved Ones,

Thank you very much for coming today. I am glad for this unique opportunity to share some of my last thoughts with you. When I think back over the last months and years, I think of the love and support that so many people have given me and my family. You have prayed for us and shown your love and concern in so many practical ways. Your visits, cards, calls, and prayers have meant so much. They gave me strength to keep fighting and encouraged me to face the challenge of each new day. I feel this struggle has not been mine alone. Many of you have shared in it. I find it hard to express in words exactly how much you all mean to me.

Many of you have commented on my ability to keep fighting and hold up through such difficult times. I want to give credit to the one to whom credit is due. The relationship that I have with Jesus Christ as my personal Savior has enabled me to continue to trust God to see me through each day. This relationship with Jesus not only gave me the strength to keep going but also gave me the assurance that, when I died, I would be with Him in heaven for eternity. If there is one message I could pass along to my classmates and friends it would be that you seriously consider your relationship with Jesus Christ and where you'll be spending eternity.

I don't want you to mourn for me today. Instead I want you to rejoice with me and celebrate because heaven is far better than the best thing this earth has to offer. And, because of Jesus Christ, we can look forward to seeing each other again.

Love, Brad

Brad's letter was a reminder that this life is not the end for the believer. We have the assurance that we will be reunited with our loved ones. Brad was a wonderful son, and it was his strength and courage that inspired us to keep going.

Joanie Cook lives in Clovis, California with her husband, Richard. Both are retired schoolteachers. They have two sons, Matt and Aaron. Matt is a pastor and Aaron is the principal of an elementary school in Clovis. Both sons are married and have given Richard and Joanie seven grandchildren. The Cooks can be reached at: richard.joaniecook@gmail.com

Celestial Conversations
By Lo Anne Mayer

Our daughter, Cyndi, died on July 19, 2005, by suicide. My journey from shock and disbelief to healing and honoring our daughter's life has taken time and forgiveness of myself and others. As I look back, I have learned some things that might help parents who are raising children, as well as those who have lost a child. The journey has been challenging but the result has expanded my soul.

Cyndi slipped out of my body into the hands of the obstetrician as gently as a soft wave hits the beach. So different from the delivery of her sister, born fourteen months earlier, when I endured hours of intense labor. Cyndi's soft peach-fuzz hair was golden blonde. Her blue eyes seemed at once sparkling and wise.

Taking her home that beautiful autumn day never gave us a glimpse of the challenges to come. Her family welcomed her with open arms. Four more children were born in the next seven years. In retrospect, I believe that's where Cyndi's self-esteem got lost. No one noticed. She played happily, never complaining, In our own "family daycare," Cyndi wore the face of a happy child in a happy family, but she kept her own counsel.

In grammar school, she complained of stomach pains in school. She cried when her teachers were mean to her or when anyone else was. All our children went to the same school, so I didn't respond with alarm that Cyndi's teacher wasn't the epitome of Christian charity. Besides, I was exhausted most of the time. There were six rambunctious kids in the family and very little sleep for me.

High school began the nightmare for Cyndi. She was listed in Who's Who of High School Students in America because she was so academically smart. Yet her friends were the known troublemakers in school. We came down hard on her— grounding, threatening, and watching her every move. It made no difference. One day, her sister told us that Cyndi suffered from bulimia. I had never heard that word before. I took her to our pediatrician, who recommended a child psychologist. Six months into treatment, Cyndi tried to commit suicide. No parent could ever have felt more shocked! We brought her home from the ER, where friends had taken her. A suicide watch was set up in our home. Five children and one suicidal teenager. . . I alternately prayed and cried. I took the other kids to school, sports, or Scouts. Then I prayed and cried some more.

Professional help seemed to improve Cyndi's outlook on life enough for her to go back to high school. That summer, we sent her to Germany to visit with my brother to give her a new perspective on life. It helped. When she returned to the U.S., she seemed interested in college. We chose a university close by so we could help, if needed. Within six months, she quit college and went to work at Macy's to be with her boyfriend. When we found out, there was more confrontation and grounding, but no explanation. After countless weeks of Cyndi sneaking out of the house, I lost it! I gave her the ultimatum of conforming to our rules or leaving the house. Never in my wildest dreams did I expect her to leave and never return. If I had known the outcome, she might be alive today.

Eventually, she married her new boyfriend, and they had two children. We reunited as a family. I felt my prayers had been answered. Then her second child was diagnosed with autism. She stopped talking with us, turned to her powerful husband, and did whatever he or the experts on autism recommended. When I went over to visit, she just cried and cried. No conversation or explanation.

Cyndi's husband's health began to deteriorate. He had three successive and complete liver transplants. One of those surgeries was in another state, which required him to stay for six months in the hospital. During this time, Cyndi met one or two new boyfriends that we never knew about.

The day she asked her husband for a divorce, the real war began. Cyndi had no money of her own so we offered to help her financially. She needed an attorney. Her husband's wealth and rage made it clear he would take the children from her, and that she would never see them again. Despite that, she seemed positive that all would be well after the divorce. She had a plan for her "beautiful boys," as she called them, although she never shared the details of her plan with us. All she said was that she wanted to become a butterfly "after being a caterpillar for so long." The sunshine in her eyes convinced me her plan was possible.

My friend invited me to a Writers Retreat in Glastonbury, England. My exhaustion, plus the inevitable stress of Cyndi's upcoming divorce, inspired my husband to say, 'It's only eight days, honey. You can use the break." That was all that I needed to register for the course. I never realized that when Cyndi came to say goodbye, it would be the last time I'd ever see her. While I was away, Cyndi died of suicide.

Looking back, I realize that she was sliding toward her death for years. How could I have missed it? I thought I had done all the right things. Now I realize I missed one essential contribution to Cyndi's life: she never felt deeply loved. I fed her, clothed her, helped her, educated her, fixed her, molded her, disciplined her, but I didn't demonstrate my love for her, despite her mistakes. While I know it was her decision to swallow a bottle of pills with a bottle of wine in a fit of depression, I realize that I contributed to her death. So did many others. Surviving that guilt of not loving her enough and the heartbreak of losing her has been an uphill battle.

Without my faith in God, I am not sure I would have survived Cyndi's death. Unlike many people who have lost loved ones, I never felt God was to blame. I never felt abandoned by God. I was blessed. I could still pray. God seemed to surround me and give me strength. God was truly the wind beneath my wings as I sought to understand and accept Cyndi's death. My faith was a warm blanket on a cold night. I thought of the many people in the Bible who lost children. King David stood out as someone who grew from his grief. Mary, the mother of Christ, was another. How I wanted to grow from my grief! When my brother asked if I wanted to go to the Holy Land, I jumped at the chance to walk in the footsteps of these amazing heroes of the Judeo-Christian world.

I stood at David's tomb, at the Wailing Wall, and the site of the children killed by order of King Herod. I walked the Via Dolorosa with other pilgrims, knelt at the sight of the crucifixion of Christ, and prayed at His tomb. I realized for the first time how many unnamed parents of dead children had not just survived, but grew to spiritual heights because of their grief. Jerusalem gave me my goal: to be a source of unconditional love for others. Maybe I couldn't be a Biblical hero, but I could make a difference. First, I had to heal my own broken heart. I had no idea how, but with God's help, I was determined to try. Surprisingly, I also received help from my mother and my daughter, Cyndi.

For two years, I felt healing take root in my mind, body, and spirit through a process of transpersonal journaling. I called it "Celestial Conversations." The wisdom I received in those journals changed me. People noticed. My grief counselor encouraged me to write a book about how this process helped me. While I was writing the manuscript, I began to give workshops on transpersonal journaling. It was thrilling to know that I could help other people.

Published by Cape House in 2012, *Celestial Conversations: Healing Relationships After Death* became an e-book and an audio book. Before long, I was traveling to different states to share my process of prayer, meditation, and journaling. I was invited to give talks, workshops, and retreats on healing grief. My message of forgiveness and unconditional love clearly seemed to help others. Through it all, I learned that Mother-Daughter love never dies. I now know that the loved ones beyond the veil can help us. Most of all, I learned that forgiveness is the key to unconditional love. Whatever time that I have left, I intend to be an example of that truth.

Looking back, I received the help I prayed for after Cyndi died. A mantle of wisdom and grace surrounded me. Many brave heroes who survived the loss of their child taught me that prayer does move mountains. I am grateful that I never gave up on God. His compassion is the Light of Love. I wish I had known that before Cyndi died. Now that I do, I hope to emulate that loving compassion for others for the rest of my life.

> **Lo Anne Mayer** lives in New York and is the Author of *Celestial Conversations: Healing Relationships After Death*. For more information, visit www.celestialconversations.com

New Life For Others
By Lisa A. Bright

As a young boy, Greg had the blondest hair. He was sweet, caring, and sharing—the perfect son, my second son. His biological father was never involved in his life. A DNA test was done when he was ten years old, and his "donor" spent maybe four times with him in his life.

Although my new husband loved Greg with every part of him, Greg was still hurting inside. He wondered and cried to me so many times, asking me why his biological father wanted nothing to do with him. He thought he wasn't good enough for him. The truth was his donor had four other children that he had nothing to do with either. Greg met one of his brothers, and they spent some time together, but he never got the chance to meet any of the others. That, in itself, deeply hurt my son.

Greg was very sensitive for a young man. He had a heart of gold. He looked out for everyone—his siblings, his friends, anyone who needed something—he was there.

Greg played and loved baseball growing up. He earned many trophies from Golden Glove to the fastest player. When he reached high school as a senior, Greg struggled to stay in school. He would skip school, or the school would call me and I'd leave school myself to go home and get him to school. My main goal was for him to graduate. He graduated and eventually got a job and held his own.

Through high school he met many people who became friends. Greg was one who tried to be the leader, but seemed to follow in the end. He dabbled with partying, drugs, and alcohol. These things are what eventually aided in the decision he made that fateful night.

On September 19th, 2014, Greg turned twenty-one. For two days, he and some friends partied, drank alcohol, and took many types of drugs (as I later found out from the report of what was in his system).

The next night, my boyfriend at the time, my granddaughter, and I were watching movies in my bedroom. My son had had an altercation with two gentlemen from a local bar less than an hour before the incident. Greg came home and had been frantically looking for a bottle of pills. I told him I don't know about them. His last words to me as he nodded his head to the side were, "Mom, you don't know where they are?" I told him I didn't know. He turned around and walked away. Within minutes, I heard it. It was a loud pop, and my heart sank. I knew in my entire body what I heard, but did not want to believe. It was a gunshot. I started to run outside and ran into his friend, who was yelling, "Call 911! Greg just shot himself."

I grabbed my phone and made my way to Greg. He was lying beside my garage, lifeless, yet he had the strongest pulse I've ever felt. His best friend, who was in the house, also made his way to Greg and tried to perform CPR as I was screaming and trying to communicate with 911. I remember I kept telling them he has a good strong pulse. He was bleeding pretty bad and lost a lot of blood before medics arrived. I knew in my heart he was gone. I had been there when his soul first entered this world and now I felt his soul leave his body that night. It was a profound, yet horrific, full circle moment. As a mother, my own soul was instantly broken.

At the hospital, Greg was put on life support; many tests were done to see about brain activity. It wasn't good news. The doctor had told the family that his brain showed no activity, and there was nothing they could do for him. In the morning they would do another scan of his brain.

Morning came, and the doctor, once again, said his brain was dead. It was destroyed beyond repair. My son was kept on life support while they found recipients for his organs, as he was an organ donor. I stayed with him along with many family and friends until he was moved to Cleveland for the transplants. He looked so peaceful, as if he were asleep. I wanted him to wake up so badly. I begged God and made promises and tried to barter with God to let me have my son back. Nothing worked. Greg was gone. My third child was officially pronounced dead.

Greg had died by suicide, but let me tell you this: it's not a selfish act. I believe, and have since learned, that someone who dies by suicide just wants their own pain to stop. They want to stop suffering from whatever it is they hide or have inside of them. They are not thinking about how the pain is transferred to everyone else when they are gone. I love my son and wish I had known the extent of his pain, the extent of his addictions. I would have done anything for him, anything to prevent that night. Unfortunately, he worried about everyone else, and, in the end, he didn't worry enough about himself.

When he first passed away, I couldn't cope at all. Every day was a living hell. It took me about a year and a half to seek help. I went to counseling at a crisis center and was diagnosed with PTSD. That explained so much to me. I was there the night my son took his life and continued to relive that moment over and over again. It was like my brain would not allow me to move forward, and I was instantly back in that moment.

As difficult as it was, I had to make the decision to live for my other children and my grandchildren. If it wasn't for them, I truly think I would have joined Greg.

There are a few things that have helped me cope with his loss. I attend a yearly suicide walk to help raise awareness and money towards suicide prevention. I also attend the organ donation walk each year.

I also talk about Greg all the time. There seems to be a big misconception that bereaved parents don't want to talk about the child they lost. I don't want him to be forgotten, so when others speak of Greg, it helps me heal to know that others are thinking of him. That's probably the most meaningful thing anyone can do—to talk with me about Greg, not act like it never happened.

Each year, on the anniversary of his death, we hold a candlelight vigil. On his birthday, we go to dinner at his favorite restaurant. I'm a member of the organ donation network on Facebook, as well as Lifebanc. Lifebanc is still a huge help for me.

I personally sought help through any book I could find on suicide. I spoke to anyone who was impacted or touched by suicide. There needs to be a greater awareness about suicide and signs to look for. There also needs to be more awareness about how drugs are reaching our kids at a younger age. Maybe the awareness needs to start in schools, not just homes. Our youth suffer from peer pressure, and there is easy access to drugs everywhere. Adults need to help define the severe dangers of drug use and how easily anyone can die. Most youths believe they are indestructible, so the more people who hear Greg's story, the more chance that someone else can be saved from the same tragedy.

I have a shrine in a beautiful cabinet filled with his belongings, so it's a tangible place I can visit and feel him there. It helps me see his life every day. I have a poster-size photo of him by my bed, so I see him when I go to sleep and when I wake up.

I have some peace in understanding that Greg was still a hero in the end. He saved four lives and helped over fifty from his organ donation. He donated his heart, lungs, one kidney, his liver, bones, and tissue. Had he lived, none of those other people would have. I've even had contact with some of my son's organ recipients. I met the beautiful young woman who has his heart, or, now I say, *their* heart. It was a beautiful thing to think that his heart is alive inside someone else. It still felt that his life was serving a bigger purpose than his death. When I hit a low point, I try to focus on that.

I personally did not choose drugs, alcohol, or self-medication for coping with the loss of Greg. I know that it's a trap that many parents can fall into during the coping process of losing a child, but it's not a solution and will never bring him back. I have to take care of myself, knowing that my son doesn't need me, but others do. My life will never be the same, but I'm slowly learning to live this different life without him. I never knew I could actually be alive with a hole in my heart.

I love and miss my son beyond any human words. My life has forever changed since he died. I eventually brought myself to counseling, and by the grace of God and faith, I've made it this far. And you can, too.

In loving memory of
Gregory Valentine
9/19/1993—9/21/2014

Lisa A. Bright is from Massillon, Ohio. Her three living children, grandchildren, and extended family continue to learn how to live without the presence of Greg. Lisa has become a motivational speaker for suicide awareness and prevention. She can be reached at lashankle@yahoo.com

....

CHAPTER EIGHT

MULTIPLE LOSSES

Walking Through the Fire
By Brad Lopez, Ed.D. RRT, RCP and Jan Lopez, RN, RNC

I am a former respiratory care practitioner and my wife, Jan, is a registered nurse. Our combined experiences include extensive emergency room, intensive care, life support with respirators, and burn center work. We have both resuscitated numerous adults and infants back to life and witnessed patients who died despite exhaustive medical intervention. In short, we have seen our share of tragedy and lives lost.

But nothing could have prepared us for the phone call we received on February 12, 1981. We were informed there had been a terrible accident. As I (Brad) approached the accident scene, my heart stopped. I gazed at a pickup truck on the wrong side of the road that had crushed a motorcycle. It was that moment that I realized that the motorcycle was being ridden by my oldest son, little Brad, and his friend.

My hand shook as I checked for a pulse on my thirteen-year-old son, along with the paramedic. Little Brad had been killed instantly. A part of me died just as instantly from a flaming, searing pain in my brain. It was a combination of shock, unending loss, numbness, and a no-way-this-could- happen feeling. He had been only 400 yards from our house.

As I stood up, gasped, and choked, I was overcome with pain and disbelief. I could not believe the pickup was on the wrong side of the road or that there were no skid marks on this paved country road. The boys had been riding in tandem on a motorcycle, heading north on a dirt path that intersected with another busy street. My son had obviously miscalculated their inertia when they veered into the traffic. But the accident had occurred on the south side of the road, and my brain struggled to comprehend. Why was the pickup heading west on the south side of the road?

Evidently, a little girl had been riding a bicycle east on the north side of the road and when the pickup driver saw the child, he swerved to miss her. Our son and his friend were in the way of the pickup. The driver had no way to swerve or stop in time. In the next second the two boys' lives ended—and so did a part of our lives. How did the cruel hand of fate decide that the little girl would live and my son and his friend would die?

I went back to the house and woke my wife, Jan, who was asleep after working the night shift at our local hospital. I told her our son and his friend had been killed. She stared at me in shock and sadness. While she was frozen in time, I mulled the accident over and over in my mind. Little Brad and his friend had ridden the motorcycle numerous times, taking turns riding solo and sometimes riding in tandem. Each time I told him not to cross this busy street and stay on the north side of the street where our house was located. There was plenty of room to ride on the north side. Despite the repeated warnings, he and his friend ventured on the wrong side. Oh, why didn't he listen? The accident would never have happened, and he would still be with us. Wouldn't he?

What about my responsibility? Isn't a dad always responsible for his family members no matter where they are? Although logic dictates you can't be with your family every moment—to hell with logic! That does not relieve the pain, agonizing suffering, or unending loss.

Day after day, month after month, year after year, I was not prepared nor did I know how to deal with the permanent, insufferable loss of our oldest son. How would I help my wife and younger son, Ted? At this point, I could choose to blame God and ask Him why he allowed our son to die needlessly. . . Or I could choose to ask Him to bathe me in His love and healing care. I was so fixed on my pain and suffering that I somehow forgot that God lost a son, too. But He also created little Brad and brought him into this world through Jan and me. While we trust God, He has not revealed to us why this happened. We chose to walk in faith. In doing so, we have seen God's face. Family and friends have poured their unending love on us for many years.

Even so, the searing pain, agony, and suffering did not end. There were times when driving home from work or at a store, I would be overwhelmed by the memory of the accident and the loss of our son. Suddenly, my eyes would fill with blinding tears. If driving, I would have to pull over and stop at the side of the road because I could not see the traffic or the road. In a store I would find the nearest place to be alone. Then I would wait as the unbearable agony flooded my mind, leaving a wake of pain. There was no way to control when or how long that stabbing discomfort would occur. Once the emotional wave had passed, I would sense another wave, this one a wave of comfort, assurance, and hope that made me gravitate closer to God. Only now do I realize His love helped me and sustained me through the fire.

Somehow, the sense of trust God instilled in me made me aware that there was a bigger promise, and the loss of our son was better for him than if he had lived. The sense of trust I felt transcended any logic and understanding. Little did I know the sense of trust God gave me would be severely tested again. . .

On May 23, 1995, five thousand, five hundred, twenty-three days later, the youngest of our three sons, Justin (only nineteen), died in an automobile accident. Another, unrecoverable part of me died when a driver ran a stoplight and

killed our son instantly. The pain was crushing, suffocating. . .
a living death. Absolutely nothing can prepare you for this
horrifying tragedy. Shortly after the funeral, the numbness that
I felt did not decrease; rather it evolved from initial anger and
expanded into blind rage. I could feel my hand reaching for an
intangible sword that was ready to lash out at God. That night I
collapsed in sheer pain and agony.

My mind screamed, "Lord, why didn't you give me the
chance to trade my life for Justin? As a father, I would gladly give
up my life for my wife or any of my sons. When I wake, I will do
everything I can to get even."

And yet, God turned my heart and will that night. In a
dream that night and in a trance the next day, I can vividly recall
the encounter as if it happened yesterday.

The Lord sent a message to me through Justin's voice,
"Dad, it's okay. I'm in a better place." These words reverberated
though my mind again before I woke and repeatedly throughout
the following days. The rage that had been brewing and swelling
in the cauldron of my mind dissipated. In less than a week, the
fiery pain turned to peace. How was that possible? I knew that, on
my own, I could not achieve that kind of reversal. God's love had
doused the fire.

Passing through the fire still required healing. Instead of
hiding in denial, seeking artificial means of escape, taking the loss
out on others, or rejecting God, only through God's grace could I
chose to trust Him more. This was not an easy journey. I tried to
face the losses head on and realized that facing death is another
part of life. You can let it destroy your life, or you can draw closer
to God.

But how was this part of the journey through the
fire accomplished? Although I was just starting to write my
dissertation in my doctoral program, my mind went completely
blank. Years of preparation were required to get to this stage,
yet at this point, I felt I could not go any further. I was depleted,

spent, and ready to quit. Then, in a dream, the Lord told me the doctoral degree was not just for me; it was to glorify Him. So one afternoon shortly thereafter, I bowed my head on my desk and prayed to the Lord, "If You want me to write the dissertation, You are going to have to write it though me. I can't do it on my own." A few weeks later I reviewed the first three chapters to be submitted for review. I have no memory of writing the first two chapters. Looking back, I realized the Holy Spirit had overshadowed me and empowered me to write these chapters. The first three chapters were approved. I was then qualified to complete and defend the dissertation. Only the Lord could have made completion of the doctoral degree possible. He carried me every step.

Now, when I reflect on the fiery trials facing the deaths of the ones closest and dearest to me, I can see how God used these tragedies to help me face life as it really happens. My dad died when I was eleven, and my mom died when I was forty-two.

As death reminds me how precious life is, I am less likely to fret over trivialities. Though I am not immune to life's challenges, the loss of loved ones has helped me put life's challenges into perspective. Even in the constant struggle against pride and arrogance, I daily choose to surrender to God's love.

In walking through the fires of life, God uses these fires to purify my heart and mature my mind. The best part is that He walks through the fire with me. For the part of life that was lost from departed loved ones, God replaced with His Spirit. I reach out to Him and find I am never alone. Whether I reach for Him or not, He is always there for me. He helped me understand that my boys were borrowed from Him, and now they were back home with God, their true Father.

I have learned that God is love, and that is why He can be described in one word. GOD'S LOVE: inseparable, fulfilling, eternal. I can relate to God as did Job when over 2,500 years ago he said,

> "As for me, I know that my Redeemer lives,
> And at the last He will take His stand on the earth.
> Even after my skin is destroyed,
> Yet from my flesh I shall see God;
> Whom I myself shall behold,
> And whom my eyes will see and not another."
> —Job 19:25-27

I don't just believe in God, I know God. He, and only He, is my Redeemer!

Brad Lopez is currently retired after teaching nearly 40 years in college in the Respiratory Care Practitioner Program, Health Science, pharmacology, information technology at San Bernardino and Fresno City Colleges. Doctor of Education degree 1996 University of California Davis and California State University, Fresno; Master of Science degree 1997, California State University, Fresno; Master of Public Health Program 1997, Loma Linda University; Associate of Science in Respiratory Care degree, Loma Linda University, Bachelor of Arts degree and Dean's List 1971, California State University, Fresno.

He is currently the leader of the Prayer Tent ministry in Fresno, California and the Youth Pizza Forum to strengthen and win back our youth who walk away from their faith in Jesus Christ.

Jan Lopez is retired after being a nurse for nearly thirty-five years. She earned her Associate in Nursing degree, Fresno City College, psychiatric nursing, and medical care Valley Medical Center; newborn nursery, Loma Linda University Medical Center and St. Agnes Medical Center.

Brad and Jan Lopez can be reached at janbrad50@gmail.com

When Four Becomes One
By Elly Sutherland

The bottom started to fall out of my near-perfect life as a pastor's wife and a mother in the summer of 2003. My husband of twenty-three years asked for a divorce.

Little did I know then, that was just the beginning of my painful journey.

The following March, in 2004, my eldest child, Rachel, was driving to the Florida Keys for Spring Break with five friends from the University. I received a phone call early on a Saturday morning to say there had been an accident.

The message was, "Rachel and Matt are hurt the most." I knew right then that she was gone. I cannot explain it, but there was some kind of disconnect deep within my gut. About three hours later, the sheriff's deputy came to the door and confirmed my worst fears.

My son, James, had a hard time recovering from his sister's death. He battled addiction for years. After thirty years in the United States, I returned to England to spend time with my family. He and I both hoped he would get himself together enough to eventually join me.

We weathered this unchartered territory of addiction and relapse for ten years. I tried not to think of also losing him. Then one Monday in February of 2014, I left work with a fear that something was wrong. It was an oddly familiar, sinking feeling in my stomach and my spirit. I had not heard from James all weekend; unusual because we normally spoke almost daily. I messaged my friend and asked him to go and check on James. As I hit the send button, the same feeling from twelve years earlier flooded over me because I already knew that James was gone. A few hours later my sister came to the door and confirmed that my son was dead.

Some days it's hard to believe that what was once a family of four is now just me. My role as a wife is gone. My role as a mother is gone. I am in the process of finding a new normal. Going through grief like this twice is unthinkable. Some days it feels like I'm walking through jello. I share my grief journey openly in the hope of helping others. I am actively involved in grief support groups for parents who have lost children. I worked with a reporter who published an article about my son to help dispel the stigma of addiction.

I find reaching out to others to be very healing. I work in healthcare as a nurse, and caring for my patients takes my mind away from my personal pain. I think I have more compassion these days. My faith is my rock. I feel God's grace surrounding me every day through the support and love of friends and family. I rarely worry about tomorrow. They say life is made up of moments, so I strive to appreciate them one at a time, no matter how big or small they seem.

If I look at the big picture, or list all of my painful experiences one at a time, it is overwhelming. Living the rest of my days without Rachel and James—knowing there will never be the excitement of expecting them home for holidays, hearing "mom" at the other end of the phone, enjoying no weddings or grandchildren to spoil—makes me feel incredibly broken some days. I counter this by trying to reach deep within myself to find the beauty in the ordinary, and, in that way, strive for reasonable happiness.

My latest therapy is photography, which allows me to constantly search for that beauty. Who knew that flowers, waves, buildings, hills, and skies would be so appreciated? I love the art involved in photography, but mostly it reminds me that, in spite of all my losses, the world is still a beautiful place.

And it is.

This is one of the many Bible verses that has given me hope over the years:

"Therefore, since we are justified by faith, we have peace with God through our Lord Jesus Christ, through whom we have obtained access to this grace in which we stand; and we boast in our hope of sharing the glory of God.

And not only that, but we also boast in our sufferings, knowing that suffering produces endurance, and endurance produces character, and character produces hope, and hope does not disappoint us, because God's love has been poured into our hearts through the Holy Spirit that has been given to us."—Romans 5:1-5

When I feel good, I run with it. But when the darkness pervades, I just rest and push through it until I feel brighter. I have had to learn to trust myself and my feelings and not ignore them. Laughter is the best medicine, and, though it's hard to do at times, I try to smile as much as possible. And hope—I always have hope. Hope is also a choice, but not an optional one. If we give up hope, then we give up living.

My children left with me (and those their lives touched) an abundance of love. I feel their loving presence every day. Every now and then I'm pretty certain I hear them saying, "Keep going, Momma. You got this."

> **Elly Sutherland** lives in England, her country of birth. Previously, she lived in the United States and her children were both born there. Their ashes are buried in Kentucky. Elly is a nurse in health services and has found joy in helping to heal others. She enjoys writing, reading, photography, and cooking. She also finds solace in the sea. Elly can be reached via email: elly.ertelmedpeds@gmail.com

Making a Family God's Way
By Cora Merkley

I was fifteen years old and tried to digest everything my mom and the doctor were telling me. They were saying I should never plan on having kids. What? How could that be? Ever since I was a little girl, for as long as I could remember, when I was asked what I wanted to be when I grew up, it was always the same answer, "A mom, of course!"

My mom looked at me with fear and worry all over her face as she tried to explain how great this was, and how I would never have to worry about my body getting fat or ruined from pregnancy, how I would have opportunities others only dream of. She was trying to convince us both. I was trying to absorb how this worked. . . Did I tell a guy on the first date, "Hey, by the way I can't have kids," or do I wait until I am engaged? The fear and doubts came flooding in. Will anyone even want me? Am I damaged goods? What will I become? The only thing I knew for sure was that my life had just changed, and I was supposed to simply accept it.

Fast forward eight years and I had found the love of my life, Heath. He loved all of me, even the broken parts. It gets better. He was adopted and was totally open to us adopting kids when we were ready. We made huge plans of getting married and me supporting him through medical school.

Soon after we married, I felt ill. I couldn't understand why I felt so terrible. What was wrong with me? I finally decided to just see, from what I read, if it was how women feel who are pregnant. I told myself that we all know I am not one of them, though. I didn't even take birth control; I was so certain.

Turns out, I was wrong; we were all wrong. I was pregnant. I was pregnant!? How could that be? We were so excited that we didn't wait the secret amount of time to tell people. We screamed it from the rooftops! I am pregnant! We had just gotten married weeks ago, and now we were making a family. The joy we felt was unreal. We had been blessed by God to add a beautiful spirit to our family—to love forever.

We went to our eleven-week appointment, just after Thanksgiving, having seen all the family and celebrated with everyone. Happy and joyful, I watched them start the ultrasound. Everyone was talking. The room grew a little quieter and quieter.

Pretty soon, the doctor was concentrating real hard on something and looked at me. There was no heartbeat; my miracle was gone. My baby's spirit was gone. I cried and cried. Oh, how my heart broke! Heath, my husband, cried with me. We were so young and were already going through such hard things together.

They told us they wanted me to carry the baby until my body naturally miscarried. They suspected it would happen quickly. Nearly three weeks went by, and I was still carrying my dead baby. I could not take it another day. The grief was too much. They did a D&C and told me to rest. Everyone told me to rest. I heard over and over how lucky I was because we now knew I could get pregnant. I didn't feel lucky; I felt cheated. I felt like life just screwed me over and was laughing at me.

I prayed long hours; I turned to scriptures for peace, and I found it. I discovered peace in knowing I had not lost my baby; my precious child would still be mine to love for eternity in the time to come. My job was to live ready and worthy to be with my baby again.

Just as I was feeling refocused and ready to accept what we were dealing with, it was back. Could it be? No, I must have a flu. It's only been two months, and we were not trying to do this again so soon. However, the carrots I was eating did not lie, and they were not going to stay down no matter what. I took the test. I was at work and took three more. All positive. What do I do? Do I tell Heath and get his hopes up again? What can I possibly do to make this any different from two months ago? Can I really handle losing another baby again so soon? I ultimately knew I could not carry this information alone and told Heath right away. We tried to stay calm and not get our hopes up, but we wanted this so bad.

Soon, almost right away, the spotting began. We all know what that meant. My heart was crushing into my chest; I was crying already. We went to the doctor, and they told me we just had to be patient, but would do an ultrasound to see how it looked. This time they didn't start out laughing and talking; it was straight to business. I watch them looking hard, really hard. Then I saw it. The relief flooded over his face. There in my womb was a heartbeat. My baby was alive! This baby was still there. We did several tests and repeated tests; my spotting never stopped. I was put on bed rest for the duration. I continued to bleed and feared the reality that, at any moment, at any appointment, they were going to tell us there was no longer a heartbeat.

We were told that, due to my childhood issues we discovered years ago, the chances of me now carrying full term were highly unlikely. I remained on bed rest. Heath and I prayed for our little boy every single night. I cried and agonized over my little boy, I was so scared of losing him, but ultimately I knew if I put my faith in God, all would be as it should. When I got to thirty-two weeks, my doctor actually wept. He truly never believed I would carry him this long. We made it all the way to thirty-eight weeks before I was taken back for an emergency C-section. As they pulled this beautiful boy up and over the curtain, Heath and I bawled. We had felt and known a great miracle, and there was no question it was the hand of God.

Fast-forward almost two years, and there it was again. It had been awhile since I had felt that feeling. I was used to feeling exhausted and tired—I was the mother of a little guy that never stopped. This was different, but oddly familiar. You guessed it; I was pregnant. We were feeling ready for another blessing of life to add to our family. Sure, we were poor, and we were saving to move for medical school, but we wanted our son to have a sibling. We were excited. We were only seven weeks along, though, so we decided to try and keep this one under wraps a little better then we had in the past. It was Christmas Eve, and Heath, my friend Leann, and I were off to do a Sub for Santa. Leann's husband would stay with the kids while they slept. It was about 1:30 a.m., and we had just finished. We were giddy and excited, talking about all we had just done while stopped at the light. Crash! A drunk driver had just hit us hard. She wasn't just a little drunk;

she was utterly and completely intoxicated. I knew in a moment it was bad. I could feel it inside of me. There was whiplash, torn ligaments, etc. We were sore for days, in so much pain. Soon after, the bleeding began, only this time it wasn't just spotting. I was losing yet another baby.

How does one respond to this? Who's fault was it? Was it the wreck? Was it divine intervention or a human lapse in judgment? Was it going to happen, no matter what? Shouldn't I have been happy that the rest of us survived? I had so many questions. I wanted to fall apart, but I had a baby, I had a son. Everyone kept telling me to count my blessings because I was never supposed to have one baby and I had him. I felt blessed; I felt enormous debts of gratitude for my beautiful son, but I still felt another big loss.

I begin to feel cramping in my hands, and I couldn't open my hands or move my left arm. We assumed it was nerve issues from the wreck. I went to a neurologist, and they decided to run an MRI for more answers. We got answers we were not expecting. I had a significant lesion on my C2 vertebrate of my spine. They told me it looked like I had multiple sclerosis. It seemed I couldn't keep up with the curve balls we kept getting. I couldn't even hold my son because of the pain from my accident—and now this.

Our family decided to do a day of fasting and prayer before they did the repeat scan with contrast for which they prepared me with the analogy that my brain would probably light up like a Christmas Tree. I was given a blessing of comfort and assurance that the Lord was not ready for me to have MS, and that I had duties of a mother to still fulfill.

I had my repeat scan. By then, my hands had returned to normal, and the paralyzing effects I had been having were gone. Not only did they not find any additional lesions, but also the one that had been as clear as the noonday sun on the previous scan was gone. GONE! The doctor came back to me with the results. He had me come in to the office, and he didn't just give an all clear over the phone. Before telling us anything, he asked if we were "prayer people"? I replied that "Yes, we were," and that our entire family had prayed together over this. He then stated that it was the only possible answer to what he was about to tell me. The lesion was gone, and they could not see anything else that would lead them to believe that I had anything to worry about. Again, God had blessed our lives and our family.

Not long after that, it was back. I knew this time; I didn't question and talk it away. I was pregnant! We did our best to do things right; we took great care, but, alas, the spotting began. Why could I not just have a normal pregnancy? Back onto bed rest I went, and through a very long eight months, we continued with a scary, day-by-day fear of the unknown. The bleeding never really went away, just was a little less on some days—never enough to be losing the baby, but always there.

I was thirty-five weeks when the contractions begin. I didn't think much about them; it was way too soon so they must be Braxton Hicks. I mentioned this to Heath, and he concurred. I mentioned a little something every time I felt it. Pretty soon Heath said, "I think you are in labor." I couldn't imagine he was right, but I started to pay attention to the timing. Sure enough, these were close together, too close. We were back for another emergency C-Section. The tears were falling. It was too soon. . . much too soon. My baby was not supposed to come yet. We already knew this was another boy, and we knew he was supposed to be our son's little brother. I was so scared. They lifted him up over the curtain, and I had to ask if that was my baby because he looked so healthy and strong. It was our baby, our beautiful little boy! We did it! With God's help, we had two amazing little boys.

Two years later, we moved to Michigan for medical school. We were all on our own, and I was pregnant again. Our youngest son was almost two, so it meant we would have three boys all two years apart. We were still very poor, but we knew as long as we had God in our lives, we could overcome anything. I was nineteen weeks along, and suddenly started spotting. We had literally just gotten unpacked and settled in, and it began. The spotting had increased just slightly, but I had this distinct feeling inside of me that something was very wrong. I called the doctor's office and insisted that I needed to be seen.

When I got there, they were doing the happy chatter, and then it stopped. From previous experience, I knew that it was not good when that happened. Then the technician was measuring and clicking, measuring and clicking on her computer. I asked her if something was wrong. She said it was just her job to take the pictures not to interpret them. I knew something was wrong, but I could see his heartbeat and he was alive. So what was it? As long as he was alive, I could take whatever else was coming, so I remained calm. They asked me to meet with the other doctor in the office that day to go over the results. I have also learned that talks in the doctor's office, instead of the exam room, are never a good thing, either.

I walked into the doctor's office, and he asked me to sit on his couch next to him. He then began to explain that while I have spotting, I have also been slowly leaking amniotic fluid. He explained that I no longer had enough fluids remaining to carry a viable pregnancy to term. I would most likely be in labor by the end of the day.

Talk about a shock to the system. I was 1,400 miles away from family, and I was going to lose another baby. I cried, knowing I had to call Heath and tell him. But he was in the middle of a really important rotation in med school, and I worried that it would mess him up. I was crying, and I couldn't move. I finally called Heath, and we cried together. We thought of the cruel irony of him being in medical school, yet we couldn't help our own child in any way. We called our moms because we didn't know what else to do. They both felt helpless that they were so far away and would not be able to get to us for a couple of days at the earliest. We had to figure this out on our own.

They told me to go home, get my belongings, then come back and check into the hospital where they could monitor me until I had the baby. I felt so lost. We had two little boys and didn't know anyone to leave them with. So we went as a family to the hospital. The hospital took a horrible and tragic story and made it as beautiful as they could. They made sure I was in a room away from other moms having babies so I never had to hear the cry of new babies. They got my husband and children a room next to mine so we never had to leave our children alone with anyone we didn't know. The nurses took turns checking on them so Heath could be with me, too. We cried and prayed and cried. I went in and out of sleep through the night as the contractions began. The nurses would bring in the ultrasound machine and let me watch our sweet beautiful baby in my womb. Our baby would wave at me, and I could feel the movements. I felt the spirit of the baby within me. We bonded more over that night than words could ever adequately express.

It was 6 a.m. on June 2nd. Our boys were awake. Heath was getting them situated when it was time. It all happened so fast. I tried to call a nurse, but the urges were too strong. I pushed. It was just one push, but it was all it took. Out came my baby. I was scared and didn't know what to do, but by then the doctor was in the room. She lifted my precious baby and called for Heath. We had another perfect little boy. My precious, perfect little Quinn. He had already stopped breathing, as he had not developed enough to breathe on his own. I held him in my arms. Heath and I cried together as we together held this beautiful baby. Every finger and toe was perfect; there was nothing physically wrong with him at all. They tell you that you can hold your baby for as long as you want. How long is that? I never ever want to stop holding him, but I know he is gone. I am uncertain when I was supposed to let go. I just hold him and cry. I finally determined that I had accepted what has happened and agreed to let him go.

As I lay in the room alone, as I had asked Heath to please be with our boys, I felt so empty, so unprepared. I had lost other babies, but this was different. None were more or less, just different. I panicked because I realized I never sang him the lullaby I sang to my other boys, and there were special words from a treasured storybook I never read. I cried, and asked the nurse if it was too late, could I have him back? They were so tender, and they brought me back my little Quinn. I was able to sing my songs and share my favorite words from my treasured storybook, ". . .As long as I'm living, my baby you'll be." With another prayer to my kind Heavenly Father, who allowed me this time to bond with my son all night as we both prepared for our separation and for the peace I now felt come over me, I knew I could let him go.

We had a funeral for him. It was good for closure, but it was not putting him there that brought peace. It was knowing he was with our Heavenly Father, preparing and waiting with his siblings for our return, that kept me happy. I had a reason and purpose to make good choices in this life, to stand a little taller and be a little kinder. I had children that were cheering me on, and I wanted them to be proud.

Our little family has moved through this grief. We talk about Quinn with ease and comfort; we love to talk about him. He would be nine years old this year. We thought we were done having kids and had looked for all the silver lining in the small family of four. We were finished with medical school and residency. Heath is an Ob/Gyn, believe it or not. We had never planned on that, but somehow it just fit. He is perfect for the job and has a perfect bedside manner. He gives mostly good news, but when it's bad, he relates. We are finally a little less poor, and we're getting our lives lined up for the future.

Well, almost. My oldest is thirteen and my youngest is almost eleven, yet Heath and I had this overwhelming feeling that there was a specific baby waiting for us right then. I was truly not able to have kids anymore, so we knew it must mean that we were to adopt. We always planned on adopting, so this was not hard to realize and move forward on. However, it felt urgent, and we needed to act then.

We began the home study part; we were told to expect a four to six month process to get finished and qualified to be able to adopt. Through the hand of God, we were approved, ready, and with an agency in less than two months. Not even two week after signing with an agency, we connected to a mother who was having, of course, a baby boy. We accepted we were destined for boys. She was choosing between us and three other families. I couldn't even believe we were being considered already. I couldn't believe we were going to start all over with an infant again!

After two very long days, we received a phone call. She had picked us! We couldn't believe it. Two weeks, and we were having a baby. Oh the joy and cheers we all made, we couldn't be happier. The planning began; we talked to the mother often via texting. She was very open and shared all about her appointments. We had discovered the urgency, though; she was already eight months along and was unsure of her due date, as she had not gone to a doctor before choosing us for adoption.

With the unknown so close, our friends immediately began throwing us showers, and we made the trips to the store to buy everything we needed to be ready. It was a Friday night, and we had just had our last baby shower when I realized how much I was already in love with this little guy, and how much I was already yearning to be with him and to love him.

Three days later, we got the call at 5 a.m. that she was in labor and we needed to go now! We had a three-hour drive ahead of us. We were so happy; we made video clips of us in the car talking to our little Camden. We got the text that he was here, and was 5 lbs. 11 oz., a little guy. We couldn't get there fast enough.

Finally, we arrived and walked into the room as an instant little family of five. We looked at our perfect little boy—little brother and member of our family. He was so sweet, he snuggled right into my chest. We all took our turns holding him, and we fed him and changed his little diapers. We could hardly believe this little angel was ours. The mother felt very little towards him, but I suspected that to be part of the process of preparing for the separation. She and I had discussed this situation many times; she had told us she wanted us to take him from her room as soon as we got there.

She decided she ought to keep trying to get in touch with the baby's father before we took him to our room in case he wanted to see him first. We totally understood and, of course, obliged. She allowed us to remain in her room with him, though. About six hours later the father arrived. We left him to spend time with Camden alone. It was a long six hours of being in the room right next door, and hearing our baby crying and not being able to do anything.

Finally, the moment was here. He had left, and we came over for our sweet little Camden. However, she had decided she wanted to keep him in her room for the one night they would spend together. As a mother that had lost her own babies, I couldn't bear the thought of her not having this last wish and readily agreed. I stayed in her room and held him all night; she never wanted to hold him. She never even looked at him, but I honored her and stayed there so she was near him. In the middle of the night, she said I could go back to my room and she would just leave him to sleep. She would call me if he woke.

By morning, everything had changed. Her boyfriend had called her and told her that he would come back to her if she kept the baby. She was desperate for his affection and help. She told us she just needed a few more hours to contemplate her decision. We waited with our two boys crying because they could not understand why we couldn't just have our Camden. Oh, how we prayed! We prayed so hard that she would understand why all of this had lined up perfectly, why God had brought us to her, and why we were there now.

That afternoon the agency called us. She was keeping the baby. I couldn't believe what I was hearing. I had watched this woman all night never even glance at him or touch him, and now she wanted to keep him. I knew in that moment that my boys were watching for our reaction. I was about to teach the lesson of why bad things happen to good people. Why had we been directed so clearly and definitively to this baby and then denied him?

The words ". . .count your many blessings" rolled through my mind over and over. Why, right now, in that moment, was I hearing that? I knew it was our Heavenly Father speaking peace to my heart. We cried. . . oh. how we cried. . . the boys cried, Heath cried, and I sobbed. We let ourselves cry the whole three-hour drive home. We felt angry for a few days, and then we started counting. We said them out loud: all the many blessings we had in our lives. We discussed that God gives us all mercy, and that we can be led to right paths, but can't be forced to take them. It had, once again, transpired right before Thanksgiving. We had the holidays—all Christ- and family-centered moments that could either define us for good or defeat us. We chose gratitude.

This was all new, so we didn't know how to grieve this loss. By January, I had changed my nursery into an office. It was tough, but for now, it was what we needed to do. My childhood friend had called just a couple of weeks ago. She was twenty weeks along, and her little girl had no heartbeat. She was being sent to the hospital. She asked me what to do? I had that moment to tell her: to grab that favorite blanket, the storybooks that matter, and any other traditions she might have from her previous children. I prepared her for how her baby's skin would look and reminded her to sing her favorite lullaby. I told her there wasn't a right amount of time to hold her baby, and that only she would know when. I also reminded her that dads grieve differently, but needed space to feel their loss, too. We talked all the way until she got to her house to get her things. We cried together, and I hung up, hearing myself tell my husband, "If I had gone through all of my pain and loss just for this moment, this small moment to be able to identify with her pain, it was not in vain." I could hardly believe the words as they left my mouth, but I know they were true. This is also why I wanted to share my story with all of you.

> **Cora Merkley** was born and raised in Salt Lake City, Utah. She has been married to Heath, the love of her life, for fourteen years. They have two beautiful boys, Logan and Hunter. She has lived in the Cayman Islands, to the far north of Michigan and Maine, and now resides in Oklahoma as they continue their trek through life. She can be reached at heathcora1@gmail.com

Unexpected Journey
By Gretchan Wheeler

It was an unseasonably warm day—Tuesday afternoon, February 10, 2004. That's the day our lives were forever changed. I was at my desk at work; it was around 3:45 p.m. and I was working on the company deposit for the day. A man and a woman walked in the front door of the office, both wearing black jackets with the words CORONER on the back.

Of course, these two made everyone in the office (including me) stare and wonder whom they wanted to talk to. A few minutes later, they went into the manager's office and shut the door, and then my manager called in another employee with her. Five minutes later, she stepped out and called my name. Me? Why would they be calling me? A million things raced through my mind. I jumped up and quickly joined them in the office behind closed doors. Everyone else in the office assumed something had happened to my father, who had been battling brain cancer for four years.

I sat down and immediately the female coroner (with not a thread of comfort or kindness in her voice) told me, "Your son died at daycare today." I didn't know what to say. I looked around at everyone in shock and disbelief. All I could think about was calling my husband. I called his office and when he got on the phone, all I could say was, "Honey, Myles died today at daycare." He dropped the phone, didn't say a word to his manager, and drove over to my office. He ran into where we were sitting; we asked where our son was and said we wanted to see him. We were abruptly told, "He's at the coroner's office; there are no viewing services, and you cannot see him." How could they keep our baby from us? He's mine. I carried him for nine months in my body. I delivered him into this world.

The employee that had joined my manager in the office offered to drive us to the daycare provider's home. Our 23-month-old son, Samuel, was still there. We couldn't get to him fast enough, and I just wanted to hold my little boy. The next few days were a complete blur: people showing up at our home, plants and flowers arriving, phone calls, endless tears, sleepless nights. In all of this, I continued to praise the Lord and trust He had a plan.

My dad (while fighting brain cancer) was a complete rock for us and never left our side. Sadly, I had lost my mom just two years prior to breast cancer, just five weeks before our oldest son, Samuel, was born. My dad had remarried an amazing lady who has been so good to us. My dad and stepmom made all the funeral arrangements and decisions for us as we were in no shape to decide on anything at this point. I had friends lay in bed with me while I cried. I would call my sister in the middle of the night and cry and ask why? My best friend even sat down and wrote out all the checks for my bills so I could sign the checks. My pastor's wife cleaned my refrigerator. I had friends doing our laundry. The only things I didn't wash were the last pajamas and the outfit and socks that Myles had worn the day before. They are still safely tucked into my bed inside of his blanket.

All I could think about was getting past his funeral to try and have some kind of closure. Seeing my baby boy in the little white casket was the hardest day of my life. I held his hand for one last time and sang him "Baby Mine," the lullaby that I sang him daily to calm him down. The funeral came and went. We were blessed with such an outpouring of prayers, letters, love, and support from all. I know that is what got us through the first few weeks.

Nothing could have prepared me for the emptiness inside, just a deep, deep, almost physical ache. Trying to explain to my little Sam at almost two years old that his baby brother was in Heaven was something I never imagined I'd have to do. The first time I put him in the stroller, he turned around (expecting to be in the double stroller), and looked up at me and said, "Where's brother?" My heart ripped in two, and I couldn't hold the tears back. This was a regular occurrence for me for a while. I almost felt as if I walked around with a sign on my forehead that said, "My baby just died." It felt like everyone was staring at me, but was too afraid to say anything because people don't know what to say. My husband mostly kept his feelings inside. He broke down, but I know he was trying to be strong for Sam and me.

Myles' death was ultimately ruled as SIDS, but it was a very touchy situation as he was in an in-home daycare and had been put on his tummy to sleep, which was something that we never did at home. Even still, through all of this process, Psalm 46:10, "Be still and know that I am God," continued to resonate in me and is still my favorite verse. Rather than be bitter and hold on to anger, to this day I still pray for our previous daycare provider. I have not walked in her shoes and have no idea the struggle she may deal with after going through this.

Through much prayer and discussion between my husband and me, we decided to try for another baby several months later. We knew a new baby could never replace Myles, but would bring us joy and help us in our path to healing. God blessed us with our little Ella Myles just over a year after Myles went to be with Jesus.

It has been a long road since then. We have walked through each day and healed a little at a time. Our faith is #1; the support from our family, church, and friends has been amazing. When Ella was seven months old, much to our surprise, we found out I was pregnant again. Sadly, this little guy didn't make it; at twenty weeks, we found out he had no heartbeat. On December 2, 2005, I went to the hospital where they took Max. I was told he looked 100% normal, no abnormalities; the doctors were clueless as to why he did not thrive. As much as we hurt, my heart was at peace knowing that, yet again, God had a plan.

One short month later, my precious dad went to be with our Heavenly Father after a five-year battle with glioblastoma multiforme in his brain. In the last few days, as I sat with my dad, I told him how much I was going to miss him. We cried together; I read him his favorite verses from the Bible and sang his favorite hymns. I really wanted to ask him one specific question (he was not speaking by this time, but would acknowledge us with his eyes). I asked him, "Dad, when you get to Heaven will you hold Myles for me?" He looked at me so intent and gave me a very strong, "Yes!" and we cried. I told him he had two grandsons in Heaven; he looked at me funny because he was so ill he hadn't realized that we'd lost Max. I told him he'd understand when he got to Heaven.

God has continued to bless us over and over; we were blessed with two more healthy boys in 2007 and 2008. All of our children look forward to singing Happy Birthday to Myles every year on his birthday at the cemetery. We also let balloons go with special notes attached and blow out birthday candles for him. His pictures are framed and hung all over the house. We only have one picture of Max, my ultrasound, but we still talk about him and talk about what color hair he has and what color his eyes are. We wonder about what he and Myles are doing in Heaven—most likely playing with Grammy and Papa.

On our grief journey, we've had good days, and we've had bad days. We have gotten through with continued prayer and faith in knowing we'll be reunited with our boys someday. I praise God for the struggles my husband and I have walked through; the trials and blessings have made us stronger. We continue to pray together and that keeps us grounded. We know that God is in control. It's also very healthy and important to take time alone with your spouse, and we do. A huge blessing that also helped us was joining with Angel Babies of Hinds Hospice. We've attended grief support groups and participated in memorial walks, which is important because we walk for the steps they'll never take. We attended ornament nights to make special memorial ornaments for our boys. Our kids love being involved in all of these activities, and it makes us feel more complete as a family. Also, meeting so many families that have walked the same journey that we have, we understand each other. I have continued to reach out to other women in their loss and feel that God has put me in their paths for a reason; we pray together, cry together, and learn together how to make it one day at a time.

In Loving Memory:
MYLES ALLEN WHEELER 10/23/03-02/10/04
MAX WHEELER 12/02/05

Additional Resource:
Hinds Hospice Angel Babies program: www.hindshospice.org

Gretchan Wheeler resides in Fresno, California with her husband, Mike, and their four children. They have been married since 1997. Mike works for an Electrical Union out of Vacaville, and Gretchan has been in the Title and Escrow Industry for twenty years. They keep busy with church, their children's sports, youth groups, spending time with family and friends, and weekend trips to the coast. They can be reached at: wheelerfamily8@sbcglobal.net

Faith Through Fog
By Renee Vigil

When I was a young, single mom, my incredible husband, Roger, came into my life. He became the stepfather to my four kids. He was such a blessing to all of us. He worked so hard in order for me to stay home with them. At one point, we hit a financial wall and ended up losing our home. At the time, it felt like such a devastating loss. Looking back, I lost a house, but spent precious time with my kids. We created amazing memories together that I would have never had otherwise. My four kids were the most valuable investment of my life. I had two boys, Ricky and Alfred, and twin girls, Lorena and Salena. I never knew at the time that I would face much bigger challenges than losing a home or just how special that time would become.

When the twins were twenty years old, Lorena started having stomach pains; we took her to the emergency room at the hospital. Our whole world changed that night. We found out she had ovarian cancer, and they wanted her to have surgery within days. She had a complete hysterectomy. She had a web of cancer that also extended to her colon. They couldn't get it all, so she had to go through chemotherapy and radiation. After six months of treatment, she seemed to be getting better, and her doctors had told us she was in remission. But the cancer grew. Within days, the doctor told us that she was close to death. I couldn't process that. I had to drive home and think of what I was going to tell her. How do you tell your daughter that she is going to die. . . and soon?

During this time, her brother was also sick. My son, Ricky, had been diagnosed with HIV/AIDS. He got it from a tattoo needle. As a mother, it was indescribable how it felt to have two adult kids in two different hospitals with terminal illnesses. I went back and forth to each of them and often felt like a ping-pong ball.

Lorena's twin sister, Salena, was there to help me. She would be in one hospital with one of her siblings, while I was with the other. My husband was working and also very supportive. Little did I know, Salena was suffering from a mental illness and was struggling silently while watching her brother and sister die.

Lorena ended up back in the emergency room when her stomach swelled up. I knew the cancer was back with a vengeance. The doctor told us we needed to take her home to die. I couldn't believe how she was here one day, talking about what she wanted to eat for dinner, and then she was just gone. She died in her boyfriend's arms.

At her funeral, Ricky looked at me and said, "Mama, I'm not afraid to die now." I knew it must have been hard for him to observe the process, knowing his life was also coming to an end. I could barely even grieve Lorena's death because I became focused on trying to help Ricky. A few months after Lorena died, my aunt died of ovarian cancer, too. And the hits just kept on coming. . .

Six months after Lorena died, Ricky went downhill fast. At one point, I came into the hospital, and he had a grayish color to him. He didn't look well at all. He was very angry at life and angry at God; he refused to take his medicine. The doctors told us to prepare for the end, and a priest was called for his last rites. My relatives came to town, and we all prepared for the worst. The next day, we walked in, and he had rosary beads around his neck. He was sitting up in the chair, very perky, and his spirit was very positive and peaceful. We were happy to have those extra days with him. His demeanor literally changed within minutes. I was happy to know that he had received Christ before he died. I found comfort knowing Lorena had received Christ as well. I was able to get him to leave the hospital and come to my house so I could help take care of him and be with him in his final days.

Both of my kids died in my home, surrounded by family. As tragic as that day was, I was struck by the beauty of seeing Ricky die holding Salena's hand on earth, only to know that her twin would be taking his hand in Heaven. It occurred to me that maybe Lorena died first so that she could show him the way.

My other son, Alfred, was living a few hours away. He started driving home to be with our family the day Ricky died. He stopped en route to grab food and was brutally beaten and mugged in the parking lot. They knocked his teeth out, stole his wallet, and his phone. My mom called to tell me that Alfred was in the hospital and having surgery. I screamed and threw the phone down. It was just too much to take in one day. Luckily, he recovered from his injuries, even though my emotional scars deepened. How could this happen to Alfred the day Ricky died? How could the world be so cruel?

Recovery

I often played this game in my head: what was worse? Losing a child at an early age or a later age? Losing a child in a sudden way, without closure, or watching them suffer with a terminal illness? I came to the understanding that I was so lucky to have Lorena and Ricky as long as I did. I got to see them grow up, graduate, fall in love, accept Christ, and live a big life. They both had had full lives and got to have beautiful experiences that we all want our kids to experience. I was lucky to be able to share those moments with them.

At least, I had a process and absorbed each stage in bits and pieces. I could try to prepare myself emotionally. I cannot imagine how much worse it would have been if they had died as babies, or young kids, and I never got to know them. Or the shock if they had died suddenly, and I didn't get to say goodbye. In her last few days, Alfred took Lorena shopping and told her he would buy her anything she wanted. She bought gifts for everyone. She wanted us to all know how special we were to her and say thank-you. I was so grateful to have that time with her and be able to prepare for her passing. She knew how much she was loved.

After losing her twin sister and now her brother, Salena had a complete meltdown. She shut down emotionally and really struggled. She started doing some alarming things. We discovered she was mentally ill. She was diagnosed as bipolar, schizophrenic, and had anxiety. She needed medication in order to survive. She still has episodes occasionally, but seems to be doing better.

It struck me as odd that the stigma is so negative for people with a mental illness. With a terminal illness, society had so much compassion. With a mental illness, there is often judgment from the outside, which is why people don't always get help. The more we talked about the mental illness, the more other people came out of the woodwork with similar issues. We were worried that people might judge her, but talking about it openly took the shame out of it.

I slipped into a brief period of doing recreational drugs to numb the pain, but have since been clean and even have my five-year pin. Secrets are about shame. When we don't talk about things or try to hide them, then people don't get the help they need. They try to hide things out of shame. That creates more harm than the illness in the first place. When we are open about it, it inspires other people to heal and also get help.

One thing that really helped Salena cope was to color in adult coloring books. I was shocked to see how well it worked, and how calm and peaceful she was when she colored in them. Her doctor saw the positive effects and said she planned to buy herself one. Salena would often resort to drinking as another way to cope with her pain, so I took her to Celebrate Recovery. It has been a helpful resource for myself, too. I still go to this day and appreciate the people I've met in that program.

I would often go in the shower to cry, so that no one would hear me. I felt that I had to be strong for the rest of my family. If I crumbled, so would they. One day, I was in the shower and just let it all out. I just screamed for God to please let me know that my kids were okay. I begged him to give me a sign. When I got out of the shower, I fell asleep. During my sleep, I had a dream that my father-in-law and my aunt, who had passed away, were telling me that my son and daughter were okay. Their voices were so clear and vivid. Lorena and Ricky were there, too. There was this vibrancy, like they were all in the same room together, and they each hugged me individually while I slept. I woke up feeling like they were still holding me. I swear I could feel that energy lingering. That brought me peace to know that they were with relatives and in a good place. It was a strong validation that I still carry with me today.

Another little thing that helped me cope was singing. I'm not a singer, but I sang church songs and hymns that somehow brought me peace and comfort.

My husband, Roger, spoiled all of the kids. He was so supportive and was so good to all of the kids. He was really there for all of us. He would take them to eat at 1:00 a.m. if they asked him to. He stuck with me, even with two children with terminal illnesses.

I've heard that when parents lose a child, there is a 90% divorce rate. Even though these were his step kids, he was always there for us. We have been together for thirty years. He is my rock, and I don't think I would have made it through this without him.

Some days are harder than others. There used to be six of us sitting at the dinner table. Now, many days, it is me sitting alone at the dinner table, a glaring reminder that I have lost half of my children.

We had our stepdaughter's young kids during this time and were raising them in our home. I had also gone back to work as a caregiver and was taking care of a woman who had dementia. I thought I was taking care of her, but her presence helped me heal. It sounds strangely funny now, but it was nice to be able to talk with her and just fall apart some days, but she never judged me or acknowledged it. I always felt like I could talk to her about anything. I cared for her for seven years before she passed away. She was a blessing to me.

I started doing things that I enjoyed. I loved going to swap meets and yard sales and also clearing out my own clutter. I bought season passes to the water park and took my grandkids all the time. I enjoyed doing fun things that made me laugh. It was so important to just simply get out of the house. I found myself stuck in a depressing fog and never wanted to leave the house. It's so important to force yourself to go do things and keep living your life, even if it's just five minutes. Leaving your house for five minutes turns into ten minutes, and so on. I felt guilty, like if I didn't live my life, then somehow it was unfair to my kids who had died. I could live for them—and for my other kids and grandkids who needed me here.

Don't wallow in self-pity. Get out of the house. Volunteer and serve others who are less fortunate. Look for resources. Reach out to other people, because sometimes people won't reach out to you, as they don't know what to say or what to do. Don't suffer in silence. I volunteer at my church in the grief and funeral ministry. I didn't plan to become a death advocate, but hope that somehow my story brings hope to people that they can also move forward, no matter how bad life gets.

It also helped us to have new traditions. One new tradition that we started as a family after the kids died is that we get together between the major holidays. Our entire family and extended family does not celebrate a traditional Thanksgiving or Christmas. Instead, we all get together between those dates and have a big family dinner at a restaurant or meet midway at someone's house (in early December). It takes the pressure off of the holidays. We also do it again in between Mother's Day and Father's Day.

One piece of advice I would say is how important it is to have the relationship with God before you need Him. It's must harder to try to find God in the midst of chaos. I did not turn to divorce, alcohol, or suicide to cope with my pain. I finally chose God. Invest in God; He is always there, no matter what happens to the people in your life.

Additional Resources:

For more info on Celebrate Recovery, visit: www.celebrate recovery.com

Renee Vigil lives in Fresno, California with her husband, Roger, and their surviving twin daughter, Salena. Their son, Alfred, travels the world and works in immigration. She enjoys spending time with her kids and grandkids and also volunteers with her church. Renee can be reached at reneevigil58@yahoo.com

MEET THE AUTHOR

© Sheryl Ashton

Melanie Warner is an author, speaker, writer, and a publisher of magazines and newspapers for over twenty-five years. She is the founder of the new *Defining Moments* book series that offer positive stories of hope and inspiration from people who have overcome extreme challenges in life.

Warner lost her own son, which inspired her to write this book as a resource for hospitals, doctors, non-profits, hospices, family therapists, grief experts, and other organizations that are the first responders to parents who have experienced the loss of a child.

As a writer, Warner has a collective readership of over three million readers a month. She is a frequent radio and TV guest, sharing stories from her book series. She is launching a TV show and a radio show to further expand the platform of Defining Moments that will continue to share inspiring stories.

You can reach Melanie at: info@mydefiningmoments.com
To submit a story, visit: www.mydefiningmoments.com

Follow us on:
Facebook – My Defining Moments
Twitter @MyDefiningMoments
Instagram – MyDefiningMoments

SHARE YOUR STORY

....

We all have had our own Defining Moments in life. Some of us might have had several. If you would like to share your story with millions of readers all over the world, please visit: www.mydefiningmoments.com and click on the tab "Submit Your Story".

Your story might inspire someone else. We welcome all stories within guidelines and themes outlined on our website. We only accept stories online.

We do not accept unsolicited manuscripts, book ideas or screenplays. If you would like to contact the author, please email: info@mydefiningmoments.com

Made in the USA
Charleston, SC
19 September 2016